Mask and Clover
– Magnetized Circles –

ALFONSINA STORNI

Mascarilla y trébol – círculos imantados

Translated by David Masse

Alfonsina Storni's forward and poems originally published in Spanish as *Mascarilla y trébol – círculos imantados* (Buenos Aires: El Ateneo, Imprenta Mercatali, 1938)

English translations copyright © 2014 David Masse

Cover drawing and design by Paul Patropulos

All rights reserved

ISBN: 061581008X
ISBN-13: 978-0615810089

CONTENTS

Translator's Introduction	1
Breve explicación / Brief Explanation	6

Poems:

A Eros / To Eros	10
Río de La Plata en negro y ocre / The River Plate in Black and Ochre	12
Río de La Plata en gris áureo / The River Plate in Aurous Grey	14
Río de La Plata en arena pálido / The River Plate, Pale in Sand	16
Río de La Plata en celeste nebliplateado / The River Plate, Mist-Silvered in Celestial Blue	18
Río de La Plata en lluvia / The River Plate in Rain	20
Barrancas del Plata en Colonia / Ravines of the River Plate in Colonia	22
La Colonia a medianoche / Colonia at Midnight	24
Danzón porteño / Big Buenos Aires Dance	26
Las euménidas bonaerenses / The Furies of Buenos Aires	28
Sol de América / American Sun	30
Sugestión de un sauce / Suggestion of a Willow	32
Langostas / Locusts	34

El mirasol / The Sunflower	36
Ruego a Prometeo / Plea to Prometheus	38
El hijo / The Son	40
Sugestión de una cuna vacía / Suggestion of an Empty Crib	42
Tiempo de esterilidad / Time of Sterility	44
Autorretrato barroco / Baroque Self-Portrait	46
Juventudes / Youths	48
Fuerzas / Forces	50
Regreso a la cordura / Return to Sanity	52
Pie de árbol / Base of a Tree	54
Regreso a mis pájaros / Return to My Birds	56
La sirena / The Siren	58
Palabras manidas a la luna / Trite Words for the Moon	60
Gran cuadro / Grand Painting	62
Ultrateléfono / Ultratelephone	64
Pelota en el agua / Ball in the Water	66
Cigarra en noche de luna / Cicada on a Moonlit Night	68
Flor en una mano / Flower in a Hand	70
Alguna mujer / One of the Women	72
Planos en un crepúsculo / Planes in a Twilight	74
Jardín zoológico de nubes / Cloud Zoo	76
Aeroplano en un espejo / Airplane in a Mirror	78

Nido en una estatua / Nest in a Statue	80
El cielo / The Sky	82
El muerto huyente / The Fleeing Cadaver	84
Sirena de buque en puerto / Siren of a Ship in Port	86
Sugestión del canto de un pájaro / Suggestion of Birdsong	88
El sueño / Sleep	90
Dios-Fuerza / God-Force	92
Alegoría de la primavera / Allegory of Spring	94
Mar de pantalla / Screen Ocean	96
Dibujos animados / Animated Drawings	98
Página musical / Musical Page	100
Una oreja / An Ear	102
Un lápiz / A Pencil	104
Una gallina / A Hen	106
Un diente / A Tooth	108
Una lágrima / A Tear	110
A Madona poesía / To Mother Poetry	112
Notes on the Text	114

TRANSLATOR'S INTRODUCTION

For many readers, especially those from Argentina, Alfonsina Storni needs no introduction. Her biography and literary milieu, the variety and volume of her published writing, critical reception through the decades and her place in both Argentine popular culture and international feminism are well documented. Her tragic story has been told in film and inspired the deeply popular song "Alfonsina y el mar" ("Alfonsina and the Sea"); more recently, many personal webpages contain a Storni poem or two, often posted as inspiration. I, on the other hand, had not read anything by Storni until a friend returned from a trip to Buenos Aires with a paperback edition of *Mascarilla y trébol* (packaged with photographs of the author, an extended preface and other poems, including Storni's last, "Voy a dormir," or "I'm Going to Sleep"). Reading through it, I was intrigued by what I perceived as connections to more widely known Latin American poets like Darío, Mistral and Vallejo.

My goal here, however, is not to trace influences or attempt scholarly analysis. It is rather to explain the genesis of this project and to orient the reader to certain aspects of the source material and how I have handled them for the English version. It should be noted that I undertook this translation more or less as a hobby. My relevant background includes only a US undergraduate minor in Latin American studies completed in 1999 and some personal and professional visits to Buenos Aires, Montevideo and other parts of the region (though never with Storni much in mind).

So why *Mask and Clover*? Judging by the available anthologies that include Storni's poetry, perhaps ten to fifteen of the fifty-two poems in this, her final book-length work, have been published in English while the rest have not. I had been looking for a first substantial translation project for some time, so I seized on the already-translated parts of *Mask and Clover* as a guide initially. The material's style turned out to be distinct – from the work of other poets and from Storni's own prior poetry – and cohesive enough to sustain interest in trying to reproduce the rest of it.

As context, in 1938 the author was in her mid-forties with her first book of poems having been published over twenty years earlier. Her poetry and journalism had become well known; her feminist stance was sometimes controversial, but her work sold well enough to eventually provide a comfortable life. Even while raising a child as a single mother and working at jobs other than writing, Storni strove to earn the professional approval and social acceptance of writers she admired – and got it, with a few exceptions (notably Borges). *Mask and Clover* was to be her eighth book of verse, the previous seven having grown steadily more avant-garde. With a prolific career already behind her, she must have felt relatively free to experiment. Compounding this freedom to ask more of the reader, but imposing cruel limits, was Storni's medical and psychological condition. Suffering from breast cancer for two years and mourning the suicide of her friend (and strong literary influence), Horacio Quiroga, Storni famously drowned herself by walking into the sea at Mar del Plata – one month after seeing these fifty-two "anti-sonnets" in print.

Storni's having composed "the majority in a few minutes" (see her "Brief Explanation," which follows) and under duress does seem to push her voice into a new and fascinating register: phantasmagoric, oneiric, satiric, dense in images and suffused with dread. There is often a queasiness of the kind evoked by the phrase "soft muck," which appears in two poems in a row ("American Sun," "Suggestion of a Willow"), and the feeling of being underwater or underground. Because nature is as contaminated as the city, animal, mineral and vegetable are no longer separate categories. This atmosphere elaborates on Storni's persistent themes of death and the sea. Indeed, *Mask and Clover* could be seen as an extended meditation on the afterlife, a personal vision encompassing heaven and hell but more focused on purgatory and limbo, as well as the classical underworld.

The direct and wised-up tone of often-cited earlier pieces like "Tú me quieres blanca" ("You Want Me Pure White") returns from time to time (see "Plea to Prometheus"). There are even moments of delicacy, lightness, air and warmth, but the default mode is a formal narrator's voice of foreboding. As heard in recordings available online (see sources listed at the start of the endnotes that follow the poems), Storni gave readings in such a voice. Occasionally there is a false note or a conceit that falls flat (e.g. "A Pencil"), which is to be expected given the surrealist-influenced way that Storni describes her creative process: "almost in a trance." Culminating in *Mask and Clover*, she amplifies the practice of piling up metaphors, awkwardly at times, until they start overlapping and mixing (see, for example, "Allegory of Spring"). This seems to me a deliberate choice meant to convey the perverse indeterminacy of objects in dreams (or depressive reveries).

Moving to the text itself, following the 1938 first edition, I have retained the subtitle, *círculos imantados* (*Magnetized Circles*). Storni-related publications – complete works, other reprints, translations, anthologies, critical essays, biographies and such – generally omit this phrase in paratext (except in some bibliographies and library catalogs) and have done so consistently through the decades. I can understand how "magnetized circles" might be rejected as jejune or extraneous. One wonders whether "imantados" ("magnetized") was chosen deliberately over "magnéticos" ("magnetic") and whether it makes any difference. The word "círculo" appears just once among the poems (a vague reference in the occult-leaning "Colonia at Midnight") as does "imantado" (in "Youths," where it seems to refer to the pull of desire).

The phrase "mascarilla y trébol" ("mask and clover") is scarcely less puzzling or offbeat, a warning to the reader not to expect anything typically Parnassian – perhaps comparable to Vallejo's title *Trilce* (an untranslatable neologism) in immediately throwing up an obstacle to understanding. "Mascarilla" is not the generic word for "mask" ("máscara") but rather the name for a few kinds of masks: those that cover only the upper half of the face (as worn at a masked ball, for example), surgical masks, and cosmetic treatments for the face. However, in the context of Storni, the most likely meaning is "death mask" (see the poems' only two instances of "máscara" – there is none of "mascarilla" – in "Baroque Self-Portrait" and "Sleep"). As one literary encyclopedia suggests (see endnotes, source ELL, page 773), the clover could be growing over graves in a cemetery. "Trébol" makes a couple of appearances in the poems ("Suggestion of a Willow" and "Ball in the Water"), and these provide some justification for choosing "clover" over other related senses: "trefoil" and "clubs" (the suit of cards). Nevertheless, the significance of the full title for me remains one of the most mysterious aspects of the book.

There is some order to Storni's sequencing. The first poem, "To Eros," an ambiguous renunciation of sexual desire and love, seems to pair with the final one in the volume, "To Mother Poetry," a humble declaration of loyalty. "To Eros" is followed by five poems whose titles start with "The River Plate," all of which could be called maritime landscapes. Mirroring this, the five poems that precede "To Mother Poetry" all have titles in the form [indefinite article] [simple common noun] and could be called miniatures. Groupings are looser in the middle section, with an outlier in style or subject matter here and there. For example, the poems from "Ravines of the River Plate in Colonia" to "American Sun," following those just mentioned that explore the estuary, examine Colonia on its northern shore and then Buenos Aires to the south.

I would admit that, upon first reading, the poems left only an impressionistic blur, partly because they often appear to defy grammar. Upon further inspection, however, there is almost nothing that cannot be read as well-formed sentences, however convoluted. The "Brief

Explanation" exaggerates only a little when it says "everything here has a sense, a logic, though at times supported by the knowledge, ideas, symbols that, one supposes, are in the reader's mental cupboard." Storni's omission of subject pronouns does go beyond what is common in Spanish, causing a little confusion for me at least. But I found that, unless indicated otherwise, the main noun in the title of the poem is usually the subject/actor – even if for the first time in line fourteen (certainly a normal poetic convention but exaggerated in Storni).

The poems use fairly few commas and tend toward run-on phrases connected together with a series of *and*s. I generally reflected this practice except in cases where the meaning required more punctuation to be as evident in English as it is in Spanish.

There is no rhyme scheme, but the lines are uniformly eleven-syllable. I did not attempt a regular syllable pattern in English as this would likely have more costs to fidelity than benefits to sonority. I tried to keep the number of syllables similar from line to line; but Storni's lines were very seldom enjambed, so I mostly avoided enjambment in English as well. Storni does sometimes use line breaks for effect, which I replicated wherever possible.

As for special vocabulary, Storni does not use *lunfardo*, or tango-salon slang, per se; but some of her words and phrases do seem *porteño*, specific to Buenos Aires. An example would be her calling a sunset by its Italian name, "tramonto." Several words are recurring favorites: "pomo," "alzar" and "balancear/balanceante," for example – prized for having several meanings that can shift to reveal alternate interpretations of the rest of the stanza or the entire poem. I handled the translation in this situation as best I could by picking a main meaning to get across and then perhaps shading the rest of the line to also suggest other senses. The reader may also consult the endnotes that start on page 114 for running commentary.

All observations are welcome via maskandclover@gmail.com.

BREVE EXPLICACIÓN

Por el juicio general – no de minoría – recogido a raíz de la publicación de algún poema de este libro en diarios y revistas, preveo que va a ser tildado de oscuro.

*

Yo pediría al diologante amigo una lectura detenida de él: todo tiene aquí un sentido, una lógica, aunque por momentos se apoye en conocimientos, ideas, símbolos, que, se supone, están en la alacena mental del lector.

*

Desde luego que alguna parte de este volumen necesita de la colaboración imaginativa, en cierto modo creadora, del que lo transita.

*

Pero ¿acaso la sensibilidad y cultura medias del público no están pidiendo eso: colaborar con el escritor, el plástico, el músico, etcétera? (Los movimientos vanguardistas en arte y política se apoyan en el hecho social de esta colaboración, cada vez más exigida).

*

Distracción sería señalar el temperamento de estos antisonetos de postura literaria: me han brotado vitalmente en contenido y forma, casi en estado de trance (el empuje inicial de la idea creó de por sí la manera suelta), ya que escribí la mayoría en pocos minutos, a lápiz en un lugar público, un vehículo en movimiento, o en mi lecho despertando a deshora; aunque cepillarlos me haya demandado meses.

*

En el último par de años cambios psíquicos fundamentals se han operado en mí: en ello hay que buscar la clave de esta relativamente nueva dirección lírica y no en corrientes externas arrastradoras de mi personalidad verdadera.

*

¿Será necesario insinuar que poesía como "Una lágrima", "Una oreja", "Un diente", que contemplan el detalle como si fuera un organismo independiente que toma personería por su cuenta, podrían equivaler a esas novelas, pongo por caso, que se desarrollan en unas cuantas horas en la imaginación del protagonista? Pero la exaltación de aquel micromundo tampoco ha sido deliberadamente pretendido.

*

Todo libro, por otra parte, se expresa por sí mismo, si no inmediata, mediatamente; y acaso este introito esté de más: es como si un corazón sensiblemente agitado y estallante se empeñara en querer certificar que las mareas que lo turban suben de sus legítimos torrentes.

A.S. [Alfonsina Storni, 1938]

BRIEF EXPLANATION

As a result of the publication of one of the poems from this book in newspapers and magazines, I foresee that in general judgment – not that of the minority – it will be branded as obscure.

*

I would request of my interlocutor friend a thorough reading: everything here has a sense, a logic, though at times supported by the knowledge, ideas, symbols that, one supposes, are in the reader's mental cupboard.

*

Of course some part of this volume needs imaginative collaboration, in certain ways creative, from he who transits its pages.

*

But, don't the average sensibility and culture of the public require just that: collaboration with the writer, the plastic artist, the musician etcetera? (Vanguard movements in the arts and politics lean on the social act of this collaboration, which they demand more and more.)

*

It would be a distraction to point out the temperament of these antisonnets from a literary stance: they have risen out of me vitally in content and form, almost in a state of trance (the initial push of the idea itself created a fluid manner), given that I wrote the majority in a few minutes, in pencil in a public place, a vehicle in motion, or in my bed waking up at odd hours; although polishing them took months.

*

In the last two years fundamental psychic changes have occurred in me: in this one has to look for the key to this relatively new lyric direction and not in external currents that drag on my true personality.

*

Would it be necessary to insinuate that poetry like "A Tear," "An Ear," "A Tooth," each of which contemplates a detail as if it were an independent organism that takes on personhood for itself, could be equivalent to those novels, for example, that develop over some number of hours in the imagination of the protagonist? But neither has the exaltation of that micro-world been deliberately attempted.

*

All books, on the other hand, express themselves on their own, if not immediately, with mediation; and perhaps this prologue is superfluous: it is as if a sensitive heart, agitated and exploding, were to insist on certifying that the tides that unsettle it arise from torrents.

A.S. [Alfonsina Storni, 1938]

A EROS

He aquí que te cacé por el pescuezo
a la orilla del mar, mientras movías
las flechas de tu aljaba para herirme
y vi en el suelo tu floreal corona.

Como a un muñeco destripé tu vientre
y examiné sus ruedas engañosas
y muy envuelta en sus poleas de oro
hallé una trampa que decía: sexo.

Sobre la playa, ya un guiñapo triste,
te mostré al sol, buscón de tus hazañas,
ante un corro asustado de sirenas.

Iba subiendo por la cuesta albina
tu madrina de engaños, Doña Luna,
y te arrojé a la boca de las olas.

TO EROS

And so I caught you by the scruff of the neck
at the seashore, while you roused
your quiver's arrows to wound me
and I saw on the ground your flowered May crown.

I gutted your abdomen like a doll's
and examined its deceitful wheels,
and I found, shrouded by gold pulleys,
a trap door that said: sex.

To the sun, searcher of your exploits, I showed you –
now a sad rag heap upon the beach –
before a startled ring of sirens.

Lady Moon, your godmother in deceit,
was ascending the albino slope,
and I threw you into the mouth of the waves.

RÍO DE LA PLATA EN NEGRO Y OCRE

La niebla había comido su horizonte
y sus altas columnas agrisadas
se echaban hacia el mar y parapetos
eran sobre la atlántica marea.

Se estaba anclado allí, ferruginoso,
viendo venir sus padres desde el norte;
dos pumas verdes que por monte y piedra
saltaban desde el trópico a roerlo:

Porque ni bien nacido ya moría
y en su desdén apenas se rizaba
señor de sí, los labios apretados.

Lavadas rosas le soltaba el cielo
y de su seno erguía tallos de humo
sobre quemados cabeceantes buques.

THE RIVER PLATE IN BLACK AND OCHRE

The fog had eaten up its horizon
and its tall greyish columns
leaned toward the ocean,
parapets on the Atlantic tide.

It stayed anchored there, ferruginous,
watching its parents arrive from the north;
two green pumas that leapt from the tropics
over mountains and rocks to gnaw at it:

Because, not even fully born, already it was dying
and in its disdain scarcely rippled,
lord of itself, lips pressed together.

The sky released washed roses for it
and from its breast erected stems of smoke
over burned, swaying ships.

RÍO DE LA PLATA EN GRIS ÁUREO

Respiración la suya grave y lenta
se estaba quieto, y no perder quería
el sueño, y de su cuerpo en tiernos grises
abría dulces ángeles dorados.

Soñaba una Ciudad de altos azules,
ni un hombre roto en su pecíolo y limpias
sus iguales aristas; y una mano
que *Doy* decía abierta en sus portales.

No le pesaban en su piel las moscas
ultramarinas ni las sacudía
y estaba como atado al cielo puro.

También el árbol sin moverse estaba
y el pájaro lejano y le escribían
delgadas nubes la palabra *Espero*.

THE RIVER PLATE IN AUROUS GREY

Breathing grave and slow
it stayed still, not wanting to wake up,
and from its body in tender greys
unfolded sweet golden angels.

It was dreaming of a City in high blues,
matched edges clean, not one man
with a broken leafstalk; and a hand
that said *I give* open in doorways.

The ultramarine flies weighed nothing
on its skin, nor did it shake them off,
and it was as though tied to pure sky.

The unmoving tree also remained
and the faraway bird, and thin clouds
wrote to it the words *I wait*.

RÍO DE LA PLATA EN ARENA PÁLIDO

¿De qué desierto antiguo eres memoria
que tienes sed y en agua te consumes
y alzas el cuerpo muerto hacia el espacio
como si tu agua fuera la del cielo?

Porque quieres volar y más se agitan
las olas de las nubes que tu suave
yacer tejiendo vagos cuerpos de humo
que se repiten hasta hacerse azules.

Por llanuras de arena viene a veces
sin hacer ruido un carro trasmarino
y te abre el pecho que se entrega blando.

Jamás lo escupes de tu dócil boca:
llamas al cielo y su lunada lluvia
cubre de paz la huella ya cerrada.

THE RIVER PLATE, PALE IN SAND

From what ancient desert are you memory
that you thirst and in water waste away
and raise your corpse toward space
as if your water belonged to the sky?

Because you want to fly and the waves of clouds
are more agitated than your smooth
repose of weaving from smoke indistinct bodies
that repeat themselves until becoming blue.

Over sandy plains and without making a noise
sometimes comes a carriage from overseas
and it opens your chest, which surrenders itself softly.

Never do you spit it from your docile mouth:
you call to the sky and its half-moon rain
covers the already-closed wake with peace.

RÍO DE LA PLATA EN CELESTE NEBLIPLATEADO

Alguna vez del cielo te enamoras
y lo piensas en ti; y arriba subes
y cruzas lento por el suave espacio;
y el cielo baja y tiéndese en llanura.

Y aquella blanca vela que venía
desde el filo del mar, la comba asciende;
y el copo en que la comba navegaba
horizontal se mueve en tus plateados.

Cuando el amor así de flor te viste
quien mira el cielo campos de agua mira
y quien tu cuerpo, azules de aire fino;

y no se sabe qué es lo propio tuyo,
si tus nublados de humo cabeceantes
o el cabeceo de las grises nubes.

THE RIVER PLATE, MIST-SILVERED IN CELESTIAL BLUE

At some moment you fall in love with the sky
and you think it in you; and you arise
and slowly cross through the smooth space above;
and the sky lowers itself and lies down on plains.

And that white sail that came
from the edge of the sea ascends the curve;
and the cloud bank through which the curve navigated
moves horizontally on your silver-platings.

When love thus as a flower you dress
whoever watches the sky watches fields of water
and whoever watches your body watches blues of fine air;

and it is not known what is yours proper,
whether your pitching smoke storm clouds
or the pitching of the grey clouds.

RÍO DE LA PLATA EN LLUVIA

Ya casi el cielo te apretaba, ciego,
y sumergida una ciudad tenías
en tu cuerpo de grises heliotropos
neblivelado en su copón de llanto.

Unas lejanas cúpulas tiznaba
tu gran naufragio sobre el horizonte
que la muerta ciudad bajo las ondas
se alzaba a ver el desabrido cielo:

Caía a plomo una llovizna tierna
sobre las pardas cruces desafiantes
en el pluvioso mar desperfiladas.

Y las aves, los árboles, los hombres
dormir querían tu afelpado sueño
liláceo y triste de llanura fría.

THE RIVER PLATE IN RAIN

The sky was almost pinning you down, blind one,
and you had a city submerged
in your gray-heliotrope body,
mist-veiled in its ciborium of weeping.

Your great shipwreck on the horizon
tarnished a few faraway cupolas,
and the dead city below the waves
rose up to see an unpleasant sky:

A tender drizzle thudded
on the drab, defiant crosses
with features softened in the rainy sea.

And birds, trees, men
wanted to sleep your plush sleep,
lilaceous and sad from cold flatness.

BARRANCAS DEL PLATA EN COLONIA

Redoble en verde de tambor los sapos
y altos los candelabros mortecinos
de los cardos me escoltan con el agua
que un sol esmerilado carga al hombro.

El sol me dobla en una larga torre
que va conmigo por la tarde agreste
y el paisaje se cae y se levanta
en la falda y el filo de las lomas.

Algo contarme quiere aquel hinojo
que me golpea la olvidada pierna,
máquina de marchar que el viento empuja.

Y el cielo rompe dique de morados
que inundan agua y tierra; y sobrenada
la arboladura negra de los pinos.

RAVINES OF THE RIVER PLATE IN COLONIA

A drumroll in green, the toads –
and the thistles' tall, dim
candelabras – escort me with the water
that a polished sun carries on its shoulder.

The sun doubles me as a long tower
that tags along through the rural afternoon,
and the landscape falls and rises
on the sides and ridges of the hills.

That fennel wants to tell me something
and beats my forgotten leg,
marching machine that the wind pushes.

And the sky breaks a dam of purples
that inundate water and land;
and the black rigging of the pines floats on.

LA COLONIA A MEDIANOCHE

A Sofía Kusrrow

Abre una brecha en mi pesado sueño
largo puñal de luna; las estrellas
alucinadas, rotas, desparraman
una harina de magia sobre el campo.

¿Quién del lecho me empuja hacia el sendero
de encapuchados y me lleva al río
que aterroriza el blanco campanario?
Alza Colonia, allá, su negra punta

que hiende el agua y mi callado paso
el sumergido canto no perturba
de las aves; ¡qué círculos, Dios mío!

Ay, ya rompe su cáscara la tierra
y caminan insomnes a mi lado,
lunados brotes, los conquistadores.

COLONIA AT MIDNIGHT

To Sofía Kusrrow

A long dagger of moon opens
a gash in my heavy sleep;
the hallucinated stars, broken,
spill a magic flour over the countryside.

Who pushes me from bed toward the path
of hooded ones and carries me to the river
that terrorizes the white bell tower?
Colonia raises, there, its black point

that cleaves the water, and my quiet passage
does not disturb the birds'
submerged song; what circles, my God!

Oh, the earth now splits its rind
and half-moon buds, the conquistadors,
walk insomniac at my side.

DANZÓN PORTEÑO

Una tarde, borracha de tus uvas
amarillas de muerte, Buenos Aires,
que alzas en sol de otoño en las laderas
enfriadas del oeste, en los tramontos,

vi plegarse tu negro Puente Alsina
como un gran bandoneón y a sus compases
danzar tu tango entre haraposas luces
a las barcazas rotas del Riachuelo:

Sus venenosas aguas, viboreando
hilos de sangre; y la hacinada cueva;
y los bloques de fábricas mohosas

echando alientos, por las chimeneas,
de pechos devorados, machacaban
contorsionados su obsedido llanto.

BIG BUENOS AIRES DANCE

One afternoon, drunk on your yellow
grapes of death, Buenos Aires –
you who rise in autumn sun
on the chilled western hillsides at twilight –

I saw your black Alsina Bridge fold itself
like a grand accordion and to its rhythm
your tango danced among ragged lights
by the broken barges of the Riachuelo:

Its poisonous waters, snaking
threads of blood; and the piled-up cellar;
and the blocks of moldy factories,

expelling breath from devoured chests
through their smokestacks, contortedly
pounded at their obsessive wail.

LAS EUMÉNIDAS BONAERENSES

Con el viento que arrastra las basuras
van a dar al suburbio y se deslizan
amarillas por caños de desagüe
y se amontonan en las negras bocas.

Alzan señales en los paredones
y cuelgan, en las largas avenidas,
de los árboles bajos, como arañas,
y en el verdín del puente se esperezan.

¡Guarda! En baldíos, sobre pies pluviales,
si los cruzas al alba te persiguen
y mueven el botón que se te cae.

¡No alces la chapa! Están agazapadas
con el rostro cruzado de ojos grises
y hay una que se escurre por tu sexo.

THE FURIES OF BUENOS AIRES

With the wind that drags the trash
they advance, flow into the suburb,
slide through drainage pipes
and pile up yellow at their black mouths.

They lift marks from walls used by firing squads
and hang, in the long avenues,
from the low trees, like spiders,
and stir themselves on the bridge's verdigris.

Beware! If you cross them at dawn in vacant lots,
they will pursue you on rainy feet
and move the button that you drop.

Don't lift the sheet metal! They are crouching,
their faces crossed with grey eyes,
and there is one that slips along your sex.

SOL DE AMÉRICA

Cerrada está mi alcoba y yo viajando
por las playas del sueño donde pesco
antiguos mitos y alza una madrépora
su alma futura que escribirá libros.

(El hombre, la cabeza desmedida,
salta en los pararrayos pero añora
su limo blando donde el alma holgada
dejaba hacer al animal primero.)

Por su canal estrecho la mirilla
dejó filtrar minúscula una mano
del sol ardiente que sacude el sueño.

Crecido está de luces por su llama
mi cuarto oscuro y golpeando afuera
en su cristal de fuego el Nuevo Mundo.

AMERICAN SUN

My bedroom is shut and I traveling
through the beaches of dreams where I fish
for antique myths and a stony coral lifts up
its future soul that will write books.

(Man, his head out of proportion,
jumps among the lightning rods but yearns for
the soft muck where his comfortable soul
allowed putting the animal first.)

Through its narrow channel the peephole
let seep through a miniscule hand
of the burning sun that shakes off sleep.

My dark room by its flame is immense
with lights, and outside banging
on its fiery windowpane is the New World.

SUGESTIÓN DE UN SAUCE

Debe existir una ciudad de musgo
cuyo cielo de grises, al tramonto,
cruzan ángeles verdes con las alas
caídas de cristal deshilachado.

Y unos fríos espejos en la yerba
a cuyos bordes inclinadas lloran
largas viudas de viento amarilloso
que el vidrio desdibuja balanceadas.

Y un punto en el espacio de colgantes
yuyales de agua; y una niña muerta
que va pensando sobre pies de trébol.

Y una gruta que llueve dulcemente
batracios vegetales que se estrellan,
nacientes hojas, sobre el blando limo.

SUGGESTION OF A WILLOW

There must exist a moss city
whose sky of greys, at sunset,
green angels cross, their wings
drooping from frayed crystal.

And a scattering of cold mirrors in the grass
at whose rims weep while leaning forward,
swaying, long widows of yellowish wind,
which the glass blurs.

And a stitch in the expanse of hanging
water weeds; and a dead girl
who goes along thinking on feet of clover.

And a grotto that sweetly rains
amphibian plants that crash,
incipient leaves, upon the soft muck.

LANGOSTAS

Para entoldar el cielo... no... no son;
para caer al sesgo, no; tampoco;
para aumentar el hambre no están hechas;
para hilachar los árboles... no creo.

Para volar como los autogiros
y distribuidas armoniosamente
atravesar sobre los pararrayos
de las ciudades altas, no es posible.

Y sin embargo su ala como aquéllos
gira; y aumentan hambre entre los hombres;
y al sesgo atacan y desvisten ramas;

y al sol entoldan sobre el rascacielo;
y hace siglos que vuelven sin cansarse
multiplicadas mientras más perecen.

LOCUSTS

To canopy the sky... no... they aren't;
to fall obliquely, no; nor that;
to increase hunger they are not made;
to fray the trees... I don't think so.

To fly like helicopters
and, distributed harmoniously,
pass through the high cities
on lightening rods – it isn't possible.

And nevertheless their wing, as those do,
spins; and they increase hunger among men;
and obliquely they attack and strip branches;

and they canopy the sun over the skyscraper;
and for centuries they have returned tirelessly
multiplied inasmuch as they perish.

EL MIRASOL

Le vi en un sueño antes de aquí, golpeando
su cara roma en el perfil del viento,
en una procesión de unos gigantes,
en carnaval de plantas trasnochadas.

Venía a ritmo de oso, mofletudo,
un paso atrás, el otro hacia adelante,
y el delgaducho vientre le reía
de soportar un sol sin sus farolas.

Pasó a mi lado entre pomposas lanzas
cayendo al golpe del libado vino
e inhábil para alzarse en frase alguna.

Lo encuentro aquí contándole a las berzas
su aventura burguesa de mi sueño
y fofo adulador del astro de oro.

THE SUNFLOWER

Before here, I saw him in a dream, beating
his blunt face on the profile of the wind,
in a procession of giants,
within a carnival of haggard plants.

He approached to the rhythm of a bear, chubby-cheeked,
one step back, the other forward,
and the scrawny abdomen laughed at him
for holding up a sun without lampposts.

He passed to my side among magnificent lances
falling at the blow of the already-drunk wine
and too clumsy to rise up with any phrase to attack.

I find him here, recounting to the cabbages
his middle-class adventure in my dream,
soft sycophant of the gold star.

RUEGO A PROMETEO

Agrándame tu roca, Prometeo;
entrégala al dentado de la muela
que tritura los astros de la noche
y hazme rodar en ella, encadenada.

Vuelve a encender las furias vengadoras
de Zeus y dame látigo de rayos
contra la boca rota, mas guardando
su ramo de verdad entre los dientes.

Cubre el rostro de Zeus con las gorgonas;
a sus perros azuza y los hocicos
eriza en sus sombríos hipogeos:

He aquí a mi cuerpo como un joven potro
piafante y con la espuma reventada
salpicando las barbas del Olimpo.

PLEA TO PROMETHEUS

Enlarge your rock for me, Prometheus;
offer it up to the serration of the millstone
that grinds night's celestial bodies
and make me turn on it in chains.

Ignite again Zeus's avenging Furies
and whip me with lightning bolts
against my broken mouth, but preserve
the branch of truth between my teeth.

Cover Zeus's face with the Gorgons;
call out his dogs and let their snouts
bristle in their shadowy hypogea:

Here is my body as a stamping
young colt whose bursting foam
spatters the beards of Olympus.

EL HIJO

Se inicia y abre en ti, pero estás ciega
para ampararlo y si camina ignoras
por flores de mujer o espadas de hombre,
ni qué alma prende en él, ni cómo mira.

Lo acunas balanceando, rama de aire,
y se deshace en pétalos tu boca
porque tu carne ya no es carne, es tibio
plumón de llanto que sonríe y alza.

Sombra en tu vientre apenas te estremece
y sientes ya que morirás un día
por aquel sin piedad que te deforma.

Una frase brutal te corta el paso
y aún rezas y no sabes si el que empuja
te arrolla sierpe o ángel se despliega.

THE SON

He begins and opens in you, but you are too blind
to protect him, and if he walks you cannot tell
whether through a woman's flowers or a man's swords,
nor what soul takes root in him, nor how he looks.

Vacillating, you rock him, a branch of air,
and your mouth falls apart in petals
because your flesh is no longer flesh, it is the lukewarm
down of weeping that smiles and rises.

Shadow on your abdomen scarcely makes you shudder,
and you already feel that one day you will die
by that impious one who deforms you.

A brutal phrase blocks your path,
and you still pray and do not know whether that which pushes
coils a viper around you or an angel is unfolding.

SUGESTIÓN DE UNA CUNA VACÍA

Un pájaro de luna hasta la tierra
la trajo. Inhabitada. Pero un nimbo...
Y se veía alzar desde su fondo
una ranilla humana al rosa abriendo.

Con los párpados bajos del ocaso
los barrotes doblaban sus rigores
y se agitaba la ranilla rosa
en cárcel presa ya y aún no nacida.

A luz de noche, franjas estelares
le dibujaban triángulos y cruces
de sombras y fulgor en nudo triste.

Y se acunaba sola, dulcemente,
como si arriba una celeste mano
le diera viento mecedor de flores.

SUGGESTION OF AN EMPTY CRIB

A moon bird brought it all the way
to earth. Uninhabited. But a nimbus…
And from deep inside was seen to rise
a little human frog opening to the color pink.

With the lowered eyelids of the sunset
the bars doubled their rigors
and the little pink frog became agitated
already held in jail and still unborn.

By night's light, bands of stars
drew him triangles and crosses
from a sad knot of shadows and brilliance.

And he was rocked alone, sweetly,
as if a celestial hand above
sent a swaying wind of flowers.

TIEMPO DE ESTERILIDAD

A la Mujer los números miraron
y dejáronle un cofre en su regazo:
y vio salir de aquél un río rojo
que daba vuelta en espiral al mundo.

Extraños signos, casi indescifrables,
sombreaban sus riberas, y la luna
siniestramente dibujada en ellos,
ordenaba los tiempos de marea.

Por sus crecidas Ella fue creadora
y los números fríos revelados
en tibias caras de espantados ojos.

Un día de su seno huyóse el río
y su isla verde florecida de hombres
quedó desierta y vio crecer el viento.

TIME OF STERILITY

The numbers regarded the Woman
and left a coffer in her lap:
and she saw coming out of it a red river
that turned in a spiral around the world.

Strange signs, almost indecipherable,
shadowed its banks, and the moon,
sinisterly depicted there,
ordered the times of the tide.

Through its swells She became a creator,
and the cold numbers were revealed
in lukewarm faces of terrified eyes.

One day the river fled from her womb,
and her green island that had flowered with men
was left deserted, and she saw the wind grow.

AUTORRETRATO BARROCO

Una máscara griega, enmohecida
en las romanas catacumbas, vino
cortando espacio a mi calzante cara.
El cráneo un viejo mármol carcajeante.

El Nuevo Continente sopló rachas
de trópico y de sud y abrió sus soles
sobre la testa que cambió su acanto
en acerados bucles combativos.

En un cuerpo de luna, tan ligero
que acunaban las rosas tropicales,
un órgano, tremendo de ternura,

me dobló el pecho. Mas, ¿por qué sus sones
contra el cráneo se helaban y expandían
por la burlesca boca acartonada?

BAROQUE SELF-PORTRAIT

A Greek mask, moldy
from the Roman catacombs, came
cutting through space toward my fitting face.
My skull an old, cackling marble.

The New Continent blew gusts of
the tropics and the south and broke open its suns
on my head, which exchanged its acanthus
for combative ringlets of steel.

In a body of moonlight, so insubstantial
that the tropical roses were rocking it to sleep,
an organ, tremendously tender,

bent my breast. But, why did its sounds
freeze against my skull and expand
from my wizened, mocking mouth?

JUVENTUDES

Yacentes en estratos las tenía,
pero atentas al dedo que intentase
borrarlas pues vengábanse gozosas
del ojo anulador que las lloraba.

Moría alguna y la de abajo erguía
su capullo de luces abridoras
y me daba los rojos más ardientes
y los cristales de agua más azules.

Terrible juventud esta postrera;
me alzaba en imantados vuelos como
si todo fuera un desflecado sexo:

Henchida estaba my garganta de aire
reverdecido y exultantes ojos
me modelaban por que bien muriese.

YOUTHS

I held them deposited in strata
but, since they gladly avenged themselves
on the obliterating eye that cried for them,
they watched for the finger that might try to erase them.

One of them was dying, and the one underneath
erected a bud of opening lights
and bore me the most ardent reds
and the bluest crystals of water.

A horrible youth this last one,
which would lift me in magnetic flights
as if everything were a de-tasseled sex:

My throat was swollen with
re-verdant air and exultant eyes
molded me that I might die well.

FUERZAS

Esa espada del mar en los confines...
Tiendas de luna y sol; un viejo nido
de palabras que avanzan por las olas
a clavarse llameantes en tu pecho.

Allá está el puño que semilllas suelta
hacia tu tierra y hace agricultura
de flor de fuego en tus arenas frías;
allá en el abra, junto al mar, de cielo.

Máquinas de trastorno allá gobierna
y en sus aspas de jade soy volteada.
¿Qué me quieres oh tú palabra grave?

Nadie contesta pero ordena todo;
y el rubio alfanje de la luna nueva
el vientre me penetra y lo florece.

FORCES

That sword of the sea on the horizon…
Tents of moon and sun; an old nest
of words, which advance on the waves
to nail themselves blazing into your breast.

There is the fist that scatters seeds
toward your land and practices fire-flower
agriculture in your cold sands;
there next to the sea, in the inlet of sky.

There it steers machines for upheaval
and on their jade fan blades I am turned upside down.
What do you want from me, oh you grave word?

Nobody answers, but it orders everything;
and the blonde cutlass of the new moon
penetrates my abdomen and enflowers it.

REGRESO A LA CORDURA

Tú me habías roto el sol: de los dentados
engranajes de las constelaciones
colgaba en trozos a tocar el árbol,
casa de luz jugando a arder la tierra.

Alzaste el mar estriado de corales
y en una canastilla de heliotropos
aquí en mi falda lo dejaste al dulce
balanceo acunante de mi pecho.

Al regresar, ya de tu amor cortada,
me senté al borde de la Sombra y sola
lo estoy juntando al sol con gran cordura.

Ya se fija en su sitio; ya se caen
las olas de mi falda y avisado
reajusta al mar sañudo su rebaño.

RETURN TO SANITY

You had broken the sun for me: from the toothed
gears of the constellations
it hung in pieces to touch the mast,
a house of light that plays at burning the land.

You lifted up the sea, grooved with corals,
and in a little basket of heliotropes
here on my lap, left it to the sweet
rocking sway of my chest.

Upon returning, now cut off from your love,
I sat at the edge of Shadow and alone
am joining it to the sun very sanely.

Now it is fixed in place; now the waves
fall from my lap and its forewarned
flock adjusts to the enraged sea.

PIE DE ÁRBOL

No sé cuándo... Por una arboladura
como ésta yo trepaba acelerando
y a cuatro manos descendía a tierra
la lengua alegre de jugosos frutos.

Y vi una caballada por el aire
de negra crin y a látigos de fuego
azuzar sus turbiones de tormenta
y yo chillé con voz no articulada.

Y huía; y con los otros, apretados
en un montón de bestias temerosas
nos detuvimos quietos y encogidos.

Y sacudió la tierra el paso rudo
de una mole animal que se metía
por un túnel abierto en la espesura.

BASE OF A TREE

I don't know when... I climbed around
rigging like this accelerating
I descended on four hands to the ground
my tongue happy with juicy fruit.

And through the air I saw
black-maned horses, squalls of torment
driving the herd with fiery whips,
and I screeched with an inarticulate voice.

And I fled; and with the others, pressed together
in a pile of frightened beasts
we detained ourselves, still and shrunken.

And an animal bulk that got into
an open tunnel in the thicket
shook the earth with its rough passage.

REGRESO A MIS PÁJAROS

Ya no escuché vuestro frugal concierto,
mis pájaros: que vi almenada en oro
una ciudad de espejos y en sus faros
banderas, más que manos, llamadoras.

Y en su empinada ronda grandes voces
de acústica pompal; y acerqué el dedo
y cayó la ciudad empapelada
y el aire escribió lívido: miseria.

Ya estoy de nuevo en vuestros pechos, sola,
y no es mejor que el vuestro, amado vuelo,
el orbital talante de la estrella.

Ya os escucho de nuevo, desasida,
y tú el pequeño mío, cómo cantas
en mi balcón: "¿por qué me abandonaste?".

RETURN TO MY BIRDS

Once I stopped listening to your frugal concert,
my birds: I saw a city of mirrors
with gold battlements and in its lighthouses
flags, rather than hands, beckoning.

And on its lofty patrol route there were great voices
of pomp acoustics; and I brought my finger near
and the papered city fell
and the air wrote, livid: misery.

Now I am again in your breasts, alone,
and a star executes its orbit
no better than you in your beloved flight.

Freed, I listen to you again now,
and you my little one, how you sing
on my balcony: "Why have you forsaken me?"

LA SIRENA

Llévate el torbellino de las horas
y el cobalto del cielo y el ropaje
de mi árbol de septiembre y la mirada
del que me abría soles en el pecho.

Apágame las rosas de la cara
y espántame la risa de los labios
y mezquíname el pan entre los dientes,
vida; y el ramo de mis versos, niega.

Mas déjame la máquina de azules
que suelta sus poleas en la frente
y un pensamiento vivo entre las ruinas;

Lo haré alentar como sirena en campo
de mutilados y las rotas nubes
por él se harán al cielo, vela en alto.

THE SIREN

Carry off the whirlwind of the hours
and the cobalt of the sky and the vestments
of my tree in September and the gaze
of he who opened suns in my heart.

Extinguish the roses on my face
and scare away the laughter from my lips
and ration the bread between my teeth,
oh life; and the bouquet of my verses, deny.

But leave me the blues machine
that releases its pulleys in my forehead
and one vivid thought among the ruins;

I will make it glow like a siren in a field
of the mutilated, and by it the broken clouds
will get themselves to heaven, sails high.

PALABRAS MANIDAS A LA LUNA

Quiero mirarte una vez más, nacida
del aire azul, con gotas de rocío
pendientes sobre el mundo, aligerada
de la angustia mortal y su miseria.

Sobre el azogue, más azul, del río,
diciendo "llora", aymé, tan transparente
que no hay palabras para aprisionarte,
nácar y nieve sueños de ti misma.

Baja: mi corazón te está pidiendo.
Podrido está; lo entrego a tus cuidados.
Pasa tus dedos blancos suavemente

sobre él; quiero dormir, pero en tus linos,
lejano el odio y apagado el miedo;
confesado y humilde y destronado.

TRITE WORDS FOR THE MOON

One more time I want to look at you,
born of the blue air, relieved of
mortal anguish and misery,
with drops of dew hanging on the world.

On the quicksilver, bluer, of the river,
saying "cry" – woe is me – so transparent
that there are no words to imprison you,
nacre and snow dreams of yourself.

Come down: my heart is asking for you.
It is corrupt; I entrust it to your care.
Run your white fingers gently

over it; I want to sleep, but in your linens,
far from hate, fear extinguished;
confessed and humble and dethroned.

GRAN CUADRO

Reunió la muerte el tronco derrumbado
y el capitel caído y los vellones
secos del árbol y mandó a la luna
a que rezara por aquellas ruinas.

Atrajo a alguna rata su responso
y no quiso cantar allí el insecto
y el cielo bostezaba amanzanado
sus lentas madrugadas retraídas.

Un ciervo herido con los cuernos rotos
dio contra el capitel y halló nidada
de piedras negras, dientes del silencio.

No; no era un cuadro aún para pintores
de mucho fuste, pero entré en la tela
y ágil movió la muerte sus pinceles.

GRAND PAINTING

Death assembled together the toppled trunk
and the fallen capital and the dry
sheepskins on the tree and ordered the moon
to pray for those ruins.

Its funeral oration attracted a rat
and insects refused to buzz there
and the sky, divided into city blocks,
was yawning its slow, shy dawns.

An injured stag with broken antlers
bumped against the capital and found a clutch
of black stones, teeth of silence.

No; it wasn't a picture even for painters
of some consequence, but I passed into the canvas
and agile death worked his brushes.

ULTRATELÉFONO

¿Con Horacio? – Ya sé que en la vejiga
tienes ahora un nido de palomas
y tu motocicleta de cristales
vuela sin hacer ruido por el cielo.

– ¿Papá? – He soñado que tu damajuana
está crecida como el Tupungato;
aún contiene tu cólera y mis versos.
Echa una gota. Gracias. Ya estoy buena.

Iré a veros muy pronto; recibidme
con aquel sapo que maté en la quinta
de San Juan ¡pobre sapo! y a pedradas.

Miraba como buey y mis dos primos
lo remataron; luego con sartenes
funeral tuvo; y rosas lo seguían.

ULTRATELEPHONE

"Horacio please?" "I already know that you
now have a nest of doves in your bladder
and that your motorcycle made of pieces of glass
silently flies through the sky."

"Papa?" "I have dreamt that your wine jug
is now as expansive as Tupungato volcano;
it still contains your rage and my verse.
Spill a drop. Thanks. I'm fine now."

I will go to see you both very soon; greet me
with that toad I killed on the estate
in San Juan – poor toad! – stoned to death even.

I looked on like an ox and my two cousins
finished him off; afterwards there was a funeral
with frying pans; and roses followed behind.

PELOTA EN EL AGUA

Rosada y verde de la mano tierna
cayó en el agua donde echó raíces
de un glauco más sutil y se alejaba
flor con el tallo hundido en los cristales.

Otras niñas cantaban en el borde
de la piscina y sus volcadas sombras
soñaba el agua, y las faldillas crespas
coronas eran sobre un móvil junco.

Oro el árbol y malva; azul pizarra
el cielo bajo y un mugido lento
acariciando el trébol florecido.

Y una urraca punzando y las dos bocas
a punto de morir y la menuda
mano esperando que su flor volviera.

BALL IN THE WATER

Pink and green it fell from the tender hand
into the water where it put down roots
of a more subtle glaucous color and moved away,
a flower with its stem submerged in the crystals.

Other girls were singing at the edge
of the pool and the water dreamed
their overturned shadows, and their involute little skirts
were crowns for a mobile reed.

Gold was the tree and mauve; slate blue
the low sky and a slow moo
caressing the flowering clover.

And a magpie jabbing and the two mouths
about to die and the diminutive
hand waiting for its flower to return.

CIGARRA EN NOCHE DE LUNA

Atalayada, agita la matraca
de su voz, que traspasa el horizonte
del árbol, la cigarra, y llama a mitin
a los grillos en camas de rocío.

Sobre los tanques frescos de los sapos
los grillos mueven verdes batallones.
Manda la capitana chilladora
y cercan los balcones de la luna.

Con peluca de nieve, la levita
de Orión abotonada, y muy de azules,
una mano de azufre, otra de yeso,

la luna dobla el cuerpo saludando;
y los grillos levantan, bayonetas,
hacia su reina las agudas patas.

CICADA ON A MOONLIT NIGHT

From a watchtower, the cicada shakes
the rattle of its voice, which passes through
the tree's horizon, and calls upon
the crickets in beds of dew to rally.

The crickets move green battalions
on toads' fresh tanks.
The shrieking female captain commands,
and they ring the moon's balconies.

With a snowy wig and Orion's
buttoned-up frock coat, and blue above all,
one hand of sulfur, the other of plaster,

the moon bends her body saluting;
and the crickets raise their sharp appendages,
bayonets, toward their queen.

FLOR EN UNA MANO

También sedosos pétalos abría
y eran cinco. Crecido su rosado
entre los dedos reposaba blanda
casi dormida ya en el sueño fuerte.

Sombreaba los canales diminutos
de la mano, supulcro de sus horas,
y como un cuerno alzaba un petalillo
más allá de los otros resignados.

¡Cuán gemelos sus pálidos perfiles!
Y ésa sin huesos, dócil a los vientos,
la cabeza entregada en los caminos.

Y ésta ungulada, presta a la rapiña,
con lacres de Satán y aleccionada
en viejas artes negras sabedoras.

FLOWER IN A HAND

It was also opening silken petals;
and these were five. Its pink having grown
it reposed mildly among the fingers
almost asleep already sleeping soundly.

It shadowed the diminutive channels
of the hand, sepulchre of its hours,
and extended one small petal like a horn
beyond the resigned others.

How twin are their pallid profiles!
And that one lacking bones, docile to the winds,
its head devotedly submitted along pathways.

And this ungulate, ready for pillage,
with Satan's red seals and well versed
in old and canny black arts.

ALGUNA MUJER

(Biblia – Calle Florida)

¿Quién es ésa que del Azogue baja,
alto monte, torcido en la cabeza
un sol y sobre el rostro hilos de noche
tramados y filtrando verdes de áspid?

Terrible y como ejércitos en marcha
es ella desplegando sus banderas
zoológicas, en antes y leopardos,
con sus caudas benéficas de flores.

Murallones de llanto a sus costados
levantan hasta el cielo sus almenas
negras, pidiendo el trigo de oro y alba.

Esa que viene alinea sus cabritos
en rojo labio y lo compone todo
su sonrisa que arrolla sombra y llanto.

ONE OF THE WOMEN

(Bible – Florida Street)

Who is that woman descending from the Quicksilver,
a tall hill, a sun twisted
on her head and over her face
woven threads of night, filtering asp greens?

She is terrible and like armies on the march
in unfolding her zoological standards
emblazoned with elk and leopards,
her trains beneficent with flowers.

Ramparts of lamentation at her sides
lift their black battlements up to the sky,
asking for wheat of gold and daybreak.

With red lips she who is coming lines up
her little goats, and her smile, which sweeps away
shadow and weeping, composes everything.

PLANOS EN UN CREPÚSCULO

Primero había una gran tela azúrea
de rosados dragones claveteada;
muy alta y desde lejos avanzando,
pero recién nacida y pudorosa.

Y más abajo grises continentes
de nubes separaban los azules;
y más abajo pájaros oscuros
bañábanse en los mares intermedios.

Y más abajo aún, ceñudo el bloque
de milenarios pinos susurraba
una canción primera de raíces.

Y estaban, más abajo todavía,
prendidos a la tierra los humanos
rechinando los dientes y herrumbrosos.

PLANES IN A TWILIGHT

First there was a great azurized canvas
adorned with pink nail-head dragons;
very high and advancing from afar,
but new-born and modest.

And further below continents
of grey cloud separated the blues;
and further below dark birds
bathed themselves in the intermediate seas.

And even further below, frowning,
the block of thousand-year-old pines
whispered a first song of roots.

And still further below, there were
the humans, attached to the earth,
gnashing their teeth and rusty.

JARDÍN ZOOLÓGICO DE NUBES

Quiero cantar al que se mueve arriba:
salud, osito tierno, tu señora
se besa con el otro algodonada
y cuando el diente clavas, se deshace.

Y la serpiente que me perseguía
en los sueños, está; y hay una garza
rosada que se viene desde el río
y la ballena destripada llora.

Y está el gato listado que una mano
mató porque era grande y poco pulcro
y en el tejado escándalos alzaba.

Y mi perro lanudo que se sienta
en las traseras patas y se expande
en un castillo que trastorna al viento.

CLOUD ZOO

I want to sing to the one who moves above:
cheers, tender bear cub, your cotton-stuffed
lady is kissing with the other one
and when you sink your tooth in, comes undone.

And the serpent that pursued me
in the dreams, is there; and there is a pink
crane that comes from the river
and the gutted whale cries.

Also there is the tabby cat that a hand
killed because it was big, not meticulous in grooming
and would made a racket on the rooftop.

And my shaggy dog that sits down
on its back paws and expands itself
into a castle that troubles the wind.

AEROPLANO EN UN ESPEJO

¿Hacia dónde rolaba, desasida,
por mal de ensueño? ¿Iba a buscar el nido
del viento, con sus grandes huevos grises
a punto de romper los cascarones?

Altas paredes negras me rodeaban
que derivaban lentas con mi lecho
y por algún costado de la tierra
caíamos sin peso y balanceantes.

Minúscula laguna era el espejo
que vertical se abría en el ceñido
bosque de sombras de mi cuarto huyente.

Y un aeroplano azul lo penetraba,
en la noche viniendo y en puntillas,
fosforescente y tímido asomado.

AIRPLANE IN A MIRROR

Toward where did it loop, ungrasped,
through fantastic evil? Was it off to look for
the wind's nest, with its large grey eggs,
shells just about to break?

I was surrounded by high walls
that drifted slowly with my bed
and on some margin of the earth
we would fall weightlessly, balancing.

The mirror was a miniscule lagoon
that opened itself vertically in the encircling
shadow forest of my fleeing room.

And a blue airplane penetrated it,
appearing at night and on tiptoe,
timid and phosphorescent.

NIDO EN UNA ESTATUA

El brazo recogido de la estatua
ahuecó dulce: el ave pajas puso
y erizó el bronce de flechillas de oro
y reposó. Y el ave no sabía.

El cielo abrió una enredadera malva
por aquel oro en su florón de gracia
y el bronce lo brindaba humanizado.
Pero el bronce y el ave no sabían.

Pasó un niño y soñó con la pajuela
y un desdichado lo añoró por lecho
y el amor le sonrió desde dos ríos.

Brotaba un salmo en él como distante,
y una rosa de paz como invisible.
Y ser, pájaro y bronce, no sabían.

NEST IN A STATUE

The statue's more withdrawn arm
cupped sweetly: the bird put down straw,
the bronze bristling with little golden arrows,
and rested. And the bird never knew.

The sky spread open a climbing mallow
for that gold in its graceful rosette
and the bronze offered it up humanized.
But the bronze and the bird never knew.

A boy passed by and dreamed about the straw
and a poor wretch lay down in yearning for him
and love smiled at him from two rivers.

A psalm as distant broke out in him,
and a rose of peace as invisible.
And being, bird and bronze never knew.

EL CIELO

Casas destartaladas las estrellas;
en sus camas, sin sábanas, alumbrando
el ronco animal hembra y los desnudos
sexos al sol picados y rapaces.

Y la boca del ser abierta toda
para tragar los mares de la muerte
y las guerras saltando por los techos
del solar habitado del espacio.

¡Ay, qué poeta inmenso abrió el torrente
del engaño, que pudo darme el cielo –
atroz de llanto y de miseria – alzado

en un jardín de flores diminutas,
como niños que juegan, con su antorcha,
a no toparse en el azul camino!

THE SKY

Ramshackle houses are the stars;
in their beds, without sheets, illuminating
the hoarse female animal and the naked
sexes, sun-stung and rapacious.

And the creature's mouth entirely open
to swallow death's seas
and the wars jumping from roof to roof
through the one inhabited lot in space.

Oh, what a vast poet opened deceit's
torrent and could give me the sky –
appallingly full of weeping and misery – elevated

into a garden of tiny flowers,
like children who, with their guide,
make a game of not colliding on the blue road!

EL MUERTO HUYENTE

A Raquel Sáenz

Enciende el sol su mediodía y, solo,
se yergue un luto en la yacente losa
y el mar despliega sus banderas verdes
prendido a la mansión de los colmados.

Cortan las horas las prensadas fibras
del tiempo y baja el párpado, apagando,
el sol, manchado por la estatua humana
que arquea el cuello en la nacida noche;

Y allí se está: debajo de la piedra
un seco montoncillo descarnado
en animales olas se retoza.

En vano afuera el llanto clama al muerto;
cuesta abajo rodando en sus neveras
ni en gases deletéreos ya responde.

THE FLEEING CADAVER

To Raquel Sáenz

The sun fires up its noon and, alone,
a set of mourning clothes stands up on the slab lying there
and the sea, clinging to the mansion
of the saturated, unfurls its green flags.

The hours cut the compressed fibers of time
and the sun, stained by the human statue
that arches its neck in the newborn night,
lowers its eyelid, extinguishing itself.

And there he remains: beneath the stone
a dry, gaunt heap
frolics with itself in animal waves.

Outside, lamentation clamors in vain for the dead man;
rolling downhill in his iceboxes
he no longer replies, not even in deleterious gases.

SIRENA DE BUQUE EN PUERTO

No grites más; ya sé; boyando estaba
y el perro al lado suyo se mecía
y la proa lo hendió y había abajo
una ciudad azul de hinchados buques.

No grites; sé: con el harpón clavado
te cabeceaba y desde cerca el otro
pez lo seguía por un agua verde
florecida de lirios y cristales.

No grites más; ya sé que el borde huía
del mar y solo con la luna blanca
eras tumbado como hormiga al viento.

Ya sé… ya sé… cortáronte los brazos
y sangró tu cabeza y jadeante
de la ciudad de abajo te soltabas.

SIREN OF A SHIP IN PORT

Stop shouting; I already know; she was back to floating
and the dog at her side rocked
and the prow cleaved it open and below there was
a blue city of swollen ships.

Don't shout; I know: speared by the harpoon
it butted you and from close by the other
fish followed it through green water
blooming with irises and crystals.

Stop shouting; I already know that the edge fled
from the sea and alone with the white moon
you were knocked over like an ant in the wind.

I know… I know… they cut off your arms
and your head bled and, gasping,
you came loose from the city below.

SUGESTIÓN DEL CANTO DE UN PÁJARO

La muerte no ha nacido, está dormida
en una playa rosa. Mira al griego:
no lo mató la infamia y la cicuta;
vive y sobre la Acrópolis enciende.

¿Quién te dijo que el dedo de la envidia
me rayó de amarillo los vestidos?
Era una mariposa que cargaba
polen de sobra y lo dejó pasando.

¿Oyes? Las ratas en las oficinas
no muerden suela de los directores;
hay una lluvia fina de violetas

secas que caen y producen ruido;
y el descosido corazón del joven
es la manzana heroica de Guillermo.

SUGGESTION OF BIRDSONG

Death has not been born yet, it is asleep
on a pink beach. Look at the Greek:
the infamy and the hemlock did not kill him;
he lives and illuminates the Acropolis from above.

Who told you that envy's pointing finger
striped my dresses with yellow?
It was a butterfly that carried
extra pollen and dropped it in passing.

Do you hear? The rats in offices
don't bite the directors' shoe-leather;
there is a fine rain of dried

violets that fall and make noise;
and the youth's unstitched heart
is William's heroic apple.

EL SUEÑO

Máscara tibia de otra más helada
sobre tu cara cae y si te borra
naces para un paisaje de neblina
en que tus muertos crecen, la flor corre.

Allí el mito despliega sus arañas;
y enflora la sospecha; y se deshace
la cólera de ayer y el iris luce;
y alguien que ya no es más besa tu boca;

Que un no ser, que es un más ser, doblado,
prendido estás aquí y estás ausente
por praderas de magias y de olvido.

¿Qué alentador sagaz, tras el reposo,
creó este renacer de la mañana
que es juventud del día volvedora?

SLEEP

A lukewarm mask for another, icier one
over your face falls, and if it erases you
you are born for a misty landscape
where the number of your dead swells, flowers flee.

There, myth unfolds its spiders;
and suspicion adorns itself with flowers; and yesterday's anger
is undone and your iris shines;
and someone who has ceased to be kisses your mouth;

As a non-being, which is a super-being,
you are arrested here and, doubled, you are absent
in prairies of magic and oblivion.

What encouraging sage, after your repose,
caused this rebirth of the morning,
which is the returning youth of day?

DIOS-FUERZA

Cuán descreído es Dios, que no arquitecta
cosa de perdurar y el paso cruza
de Jehová fuerte y pone en los cimientos
de empresas altas túneles de topos.

Echa a nacer un pueblo con la diestra,
y en la siniestra preparados tiene
descolorantes, y en las almas pinta
paisajes de colores y los lava.

Nada a su lengua es pan que dé provecho
ni en mar o pulga pone más cuidado,
ni piel de mundo más que de hombre mide;

Manteles cambia de su propia mesa,
que él sólo existe desmayando afirma
y hálitos le da al barro que son llamas.

GOD-FORCE

So little believed in is God, that he doesn't architect
things to last and crosses the path
of mighty Jehovah and makes mole tunnels
in the foundations of eminent enterprises.

He tosses a people into birth with his right hand,
and in the left he has bleaches
at the ready, and on their souls he paints
colorful landscapes and then washes them away.

To his tongue nothing is bread that might nourish,
with neither ocean nor flea does he take more care,
nor does he consider the skin of the world greater than man's;

He switches tablecloths from their proper table,
declares while fainting that he alone exists
and exhales flames onto the mud.

ALEGORÍA DE LA PRIMAVERA

La tierra gira y gira y va a buscarla
a un prado rosa donde está yermando,
y viene a saltos y se trepa al lomo
del mundo y latiguea el viejo musgo.

Se hacen trompos los árboles y zumban,
y la piedra cojín y canto el agua;
y aprieta el pomo de las golondrinas
y desata las cajas de las flores.

Desgreña el cielo sus torzones fila
y cuelgan de ciudades y montañas,
y un tibio, verde viento los ondula.

La mano al hombre en la cintura pone
y aguas de vida súbensele al pecho
y alza el Ensueño largas sus trompetas.

ALLEGORY OF SPRING

The earth spins and spins and she goes to search for it
in a pink meadow where it is becoming wasteland,
and she comes hopping along and climbs up
to the world's spine and thrashes the old moss.

The trees become buzzing, spinning tops,
and stone, a cushion, and song, water;
and she squeezes the tube of swallows
and unties the flowers' boxes.

The sky dishevels her row of agonies
and they hang from cities and mountains,
and a tepid green wind ripples them.

She puts her hand on man at the waist
and waters of life rise up to his chest
and Fantasy lifts her trumpets long.

MAR DE PANTALLA

I

Se viene el mar y vence las paredes
y en la pantalla suelta sus oleajes
y avanza hacia tu asiento y el milagro
de acero y luna toca tus sentidos;

Respiran sal tus fauces despertadas
y pelea tu cuerpo contra el viento,
y están casi tus plantas en el agua
y el goce de gritar ya ensaya voces.

Las máquinas lunares en el lienzo
giran cristales de ilusión tan vivos
que el salto das ahora a zambullirte:

Se escapa el mar que el celuloide arrolla
y en los dedos te queda, fulgurante,
una mística flor, técnica y fría.

SCREEN OCEAN

I

The sea comes back and conquers the walls
and releases its swells on-screen
and advances toward your seat and the miracle
of steel and moon touches your senses;

Your awakened maw breathes in salt
and your body fights against the wind,
and the soles of your feet are almost in the water
and your pleasure in shouting is soon trying out voices.

On the canvas, the lunar machines
spin crystals of illusion so alive
that you make the leap to dive in:

The sea leaks from its celluloid coil
and in your fingers is left, gleaming,
a mystical flower, technical and cold.

DIBUJOS ANIMADOS

II

Una mística flor, técnica y fría,
que es el pomo de colores, semillero
de seres planos que el dibujo alienta,
si bien terrestre, de un trasmundo viene.

Hace millares de años que la garra
audaz del hombre, por desentrañarlo,
pintó paredes y mordió las piedras
hasta lograr un árbol que camina.

Mira el pequeño ser en blanco y negro
que te calca, tú eres otro calco
de un modelo mayor e indefinido:

Un alma tiene que es la tuya misma,
la pobre tuya misma persiguiendo
trenes de viento y puerto de papeles.

ANIMATED DRAWINGS

II

A mystical flower, technical and cold,
the reservoir of colors, seedbed
for flat beings to which drawing gives breath,
though fully earthbound, from another world comes.

Man's audacious claw, by gutting it,
painted walls and bit stones
for millions of years
until achieving a tree that walks.

Look at the little being in black and white
that traces you, you are another tracing
of an older, indefinite model:

It has a soul that is very much yours,
the same poor soul chasing
trains made of wind and a harbor made of paper.

PÁGINA MUSICAL

La vi escrita al tramonto, indescifrable.
Un pentagrama sobre el campo alzado:
y era un millar de pájaros, cubriendo
de negras notas los tirantes hilos.

Se agrupaban en llaves y en acordes
en el papiro rosa de la tarde;
y a un golpe de batuta abandonaban
la partitura locos de alegría.

...Un ligero temblor del pentagrama
enmudecido al pronto en la llanura
con una sola nota perdurante...

Y era el volver de negras y corcheas
al aletazo oscuro de la noche
que reajustaba la borrada plana.

MUSICAL PAGE

At sunset I saw it written, indecipherable.
A stave erected on the field:
and there were a thousand birds covering
the taut wires with black notes.

They gathered themselves together in keys and chords
on the pink papyrus of the afternoon;
and at the stroke of a baton they abandoned
the score, crazy with happiness.

...A light tremor of the stave,
silenced at once across the plain
with a single note enduring...

And it was the return of quarter notes and eighth notes
at the dark wingbeat of the night
that re-composed the erased sheet.

UNA OREJA

Pequeño foso de irisadas cuencas
y marfiles ya muertos, con estrías
de contraluces; misteriosa valva
vuelta caverna en las alturas tristes

del cuello humano; rósea caracola
traída zumbadora de los mares;
punzada de envolventes laberintos
donde el crimen esconde sus acechos.

A veces, bajo el sol que da la sangre,
de rocas rojas dibujada y otras
hecha papel de cielo en madrugada:

Como en luna menguante te despliegas
y allá en el fondo, negro el subterráneo
donde ruge el león del pensamiento.

AN EAR

Small trench of iridescent valleys
and already-dead ivories, with backlit
fluting; mysterious valve-
turned-cavern in the sad heights

of the human neck; roseate conch
brought buzzing from the seas;
punctured with enveloping labyrinths
where crime hides its ambushes.

Sometimes drawn on with red rocks
under the sun that offers its blood,
other times made sky-at-dawn paper:

As when the moon is waning you unfold
and there deep inside, black the underground
where the lion of thought roars.

UN LÁPIZ

Por diez centavos lo compré en la esquina
y vendiómelo un ángel desgarbado;
cuando a sacarle punta lo ponía
lo vi como un cañón pequeño y fuerte.

Saltó la mina que estallaba ideas
y otra vez despuntólo el ángel triste.
Salí con él y un rostro de alto bronce
lo arrió de mi memoria. Distraída

lo eché en el bolso entre pañuelos, cartas,
resecas flores, tubos colorantes,
billetes, papeletas y turrones.

Iba hacia no sé dónde y con violencia
me alzó cualquier vehículo, y golpeando
iba mi bolso con su bomba adentro.

A PENCIL

I bought it on the corner for ten cents,
and a gawky angel sold it to me;
while he sharpened it
I saw it as a small and powerful cannon.

The lead, exploding with ideas, broke,
and again the sad angel dulled the point.
I left with it, and a face of high bronze
struck it from my memory. Distracted,

I threw it in my purse among handkerchiefs, letters,
dried-up flowers, tubes of hair dye,
tickets, receipts and nougat candies.

I was going I don't know where and violently
any passing vehicle picked me up, and pounding
along went my purse with its bomb inside.

UNA GALLINA

Una tarde de tantas. Baja al agua
la voz de toda cosa moribunda
y el sol le pone al día un lindo ex-libris
en oro, azul cobalto y rosa vivo.

No está la mente para alzar a pulso
el bloque de la vida. Vuela al campo
sin que lo cace el ojo distraído.
¿Por qué reparo en la gallina oscura

que baja hasta la playa, a los costados
dos polizones rotos por el viento?
¿Por qué persigo sus pisadas solas

que marcan lirios en el polvo de oro?
¿Esta arena, subida de los mares,
guardará fósil la inocente huella?

A HEN

One afternoon among many. Down to the water
goes the voice of every dying thing
and the sun stamps the day with a lovely ex libris
in gold, cobalt blue and bright pink.

The mind that could revive the block of life
is not with me. It flies to the country
without being caught by the distracted eye.
Why do I notice the obscure hen

that goes down as far as the beach,
two stowaways, broken by the wind, at her sides?
Why do I pursue her lonely tracks

that trace lilies in the gold dust?
Will this sand, risen from the seas,
preserve a fossil of the innocent footprint?

UN DIENTE

Torre sobre un montículo se estaba
solo hacia el cielo y tercas sus raíces
pedían tierra adentro nuevo apoyo
y relucía el mármol de su almena.

En su trapiche dio la vuelta el mundo
más de cien veces y agostó sembrados
que pasaron por él en aluviones,
ya el itálico arroz, la nuez de Oriente.

No se movió de sí que el globo vino
a buscarlo en sus frutos y dio guerra
a Rusia, Holanda y a Noruega juntas.

Cuando los vientos duros lo vencieron
y cayó como encina desgajada
tembló la tierra en que moliera, herida.

A TOOTH

Alone and toward the sky a tower rose
from a mound, the marble of its battlements
shining, and its stubborn roots,
inland, were requesting new support.

In its press it went around the world
more than a hundred times and parched
sown fields that passed through it in torrents,
now italic rice, nut of the Orient.

It did not budge from itself, so the globe came
to seek it out among its fruits and caused trouble
for allied Russia, Holland and Norway.

When the hard winds defeated it
and it fell like a holm oak stripped of its branches
the earth in which it had ground away shuddered, wounded.

UNA LÁGRIMA

No mía, que madrastra fue de Edipo
y Hércules la forjó sobre su pira;
porque mis ojos, cráteres antiguos,
por otros ojos conocieron lava.

No mía, que en mi mano la descubro
de los trasmundos áridos caída:
luna de agosto flácida y musgosa;
emparedado a cal, sol de febrero.

Ya el cobijo traspásame su brasa
pero no lloro llantos a llorado
que copia el mundo y centuplica su iris.

Y orbes lacustres tálamos de oro,
lianas de acero fúlgidas a estrellas
en bosque azul levanta de cristales.

A TEAR

Not mine, for it was stepmother to Oedipus,
and Hercules forged it on his pyre;
because my eyes, antique craters,
through other eyes came to know lava.

Not mine, for in my hand I discover it
fallen from the arid otherworlds:
flaccid and mossy moon of August;
February sun, confined in quicklime.

Its hot coal now pierces my refuge
but I don't cry and weep over a spilled tear
that copies the world and centuplicates its iris.

And lake-dwelling orbs, golden marriage beds,
and steel vines resplendent with stars
from crystals it builds in a blue forest.

A MADONA POESÍA

Aquí a tus pies lanzada, pecadora,
contra tu tierra azul, mi cara oscura,
tú, virgen entre ejércitos de palmas
que no encanecen como los humanos.

No me atrevo a mirar tus ojos puros
ni a tocarte la mano milagrosa:
miro hacia atrás y un río de lujurias
me ladra contra ti, sin culpa alzada.

Una pequeña rama verdecida
en tu orla pongo con humilde intento
de pecar menos, por tu fina gracia,

ya que vivir cortada de tu sombra
posible no me fue, que me cegaste
cuando nacida con tus hierros bravos.

TO MOTHER POETRY

Thrown here at your feet, a sinner,
against your blue earth, my obscure face,
you, virgin among armies of palm fronds
that don't gray with age as humans do.

I don't dare to look in your pure eyes
nor to touch your miraculous hand:
I look back and a river of lusts
growls about you to me, without cause.

A small, newly-green branch
I lay at your hem with humble intent
to sin less, by your fine grace;

for living cut off from your shadow
was not possible for me, since you blinded me
at birth with your fierce irons.

NOTES ON THE TEXT

The following abbreviations are used throughout:

B&B: *A New Reference Grammar of Modern Spanish, Third Edition*, John Butt and Carmen Benjamin (McGraw-Hill, 2000)
C&B: *Between Civilization and Barbarism: Women, Nation and Literary Culture in Modern Argentina*, Francine Masiello (Lincoln, NE: University of Nebraska, 1992)
DLM: *The Dissonant Legacy of Modernism*, Gwen Kirkpatrick (Berkeley: University of California Press, 1989)
DRAE: *Diccionario de la lengua española – vigésima segunda edición* (Madrid: Real Academia Española, 2001)
ELL: *Encyclopedia of Latin American Literature*, edited by Verity Smith (Chicago: Fitzroy Dearborn Publishers, 1997)
M&T: *Mascarilla y trébol – círculos imantados*, Alfonsina Storni (Buenos Aires: El Ateneo, Imprenta Mercatali, 1938)
MF: *Alfonsina Storni: Selected Poems*, Marion Freeman (Fredonia, New York: White Pine Press, 1995)
OP: *Alfonsina Storni – obras (poesía, tomo I)*, edited by Delfina Muschietti (Buenos Aires: Editorial Losada, 1999)
ORM: *My Heart Flooded With Water: Translations from the Poetry of Alfonsina Storni*, Orlando Ricardo Menes (Latin American Literary Review/Press, 2009)
PV: www.palabravirtual.com
VD: *Voy a dormir*, Alfonsina Storni with an introduction by Guillermo A. Storni (Buenos Aires: Editorial Losada, 2008)

In the entries that follow, general comments (if any) precede those that refer to specific lines in each poem (numbered from one to fourteen).

To Eros

1 B&B calls "he aquí" (meaning "what we have in front of us is…") a "stilted literary expression" (section 17.2.2), and it seems to be used most often as the biblical (or mock-biblical) "lo and behold." It could conceivably be translated "voilà" as well, but the tone would be off in English. "Pescuezo" also means arrogance, vanity or haughtiness (DRAE).
4 "Floréal" was the eighth month of the French Republican Calendar, running from late April through most of May.
5 "Destripé tu vientre"/"gutted your abdomen" is a bit redundant.
8 "Trampa" could also mean a trap more generally as in ORM.
9 "Guiñapo" can refer to a rag or to someone reduced (by some combination of ill health and moral lapses) to dressing in tattered clothes.
10 "Buscón" could also be "swindler."
12 ORM has "albinic slope," and MF has "crest of the dawn."

The River Plate in Black and Ochre

Borrowing from French, Storni – along with other *modernista* poets of the early twentieth century – sometimes used imperfect tense where preterit would ordinarily be preferred (a practice called "literary imperfect," see B&B section 14.5.8).

This poem and the next, "The River Plate in Aurous Grey," are written in third person and take the River Plate as the unnamed but predominant grammatical subject. In English it is awkward to repeatedly refer to "it" while speaking as though "it" were capable of perceiving and acting. Some of this cannot be helped, but wherever possible I have suppressed instances of "it." The three further "River Plate" poems that follow "The River Plate in Aurous Grey" also take the river as their predominant grammatical subject, but in second person, which works more naturally in English.

It seems that ochre and black refer to the river's water and the charred boats on it, respectively.

1 ORM plausibly takes "comer" here to mean "corrode," while I have interpreted it as something closer to "cover up" or "take over."

5   It would seem strange that "it" (the river) would be "anchored" anywhere. Perhaps the idea is that fresh water, upon entering the River Plate estuary, slows and becomes heavy with rusty silt (unclear whether this is a reference to industrial pollution, which is suggested in poems such as "Big Buenos Aires Dance").

7   The "two green pumas" are presumably the Paraná/Paraguay and Uruguay Rivers that empty into the River Plate.

12   "Lavadas," being feminine, indicates "roses" rather than "pinks"; but the effect is the same: pink, and green from the second stanza, streak the black-and-ochre landscape.

14   Two adjectives preceding the noun that they modify is an unusual word order in Spanish, here producing an odd descending cadence.

The River Plate in Aurous Grey

OP and VD seem to have the written accent misplaced as they both use "aúreo." Storni's most frequent way of saying "golden" is "de oro," so here I used a literal translation ("aurous") to distinguish this instance as more Latinate.

DLM recalls Storni's *modernista* tendency to create a "stylized setting meant to evoke an air of impassibility, refinement and suggestive eroticism" (page 235). Though this passage addresses a poem that appears later in the sequence, "Grand Painting," it could apply here as well.

1   Placement of the possessive "la suya" after "respiración" seems to be simply poetic usage, "su respiración" not having enough syllables. However, if there were a comma after "la suya," the speaker could be implying that the river has dominion over breathing ("[having made] breathing its possession, grave and slow, it stayed still"). In that case "grave and slow" would refer to the river itself rather than its breathing.

2-3   "Sueño" here, as in "The River Plate in Rain" (line thirteen), could be "dream" so that "wake up" could be replaced by "interrupt its dream."

3   "En tiernos grises" ("in tender greys") could serve as an adjective that modifies "su cuerpo" ("its body") or an adverb that modifies "abría" ("opened" or "unfolded").

4   The river "opened" ("abría," singular) the angels rather than their opening themselves. Since angels are not rooms/containers and may not even have interiors, the sense of "abría" that seems to work is "unfolded" ("spread out," as in a map or fan) or perhaps "unwrapped."

5   Here "altos" (an unusual modifier for colors) could also mean "tall," "lofty/elevated" or "intense."

6   "Peciolo" is sometimes written "pecíolo."

7 "Arista" is a mathematical, architectural, geographical and botanical term meaning edge, or even rough edge or beard (of a plant) or ridge of mountains – unclear which sense prevails here.

8 Unlike OP and VD, I have italicized "Doy" to match "Espero" at the end of the poem.

The River Plate, Pale in Sand

The title's word order is a bit unnatural in English, but this is meant to mimic the original, which has "río" separated from its modifier, "pálido," by a prepositional phrase. The body of the poem is fluid, partially due to the suppression of several commas that would ordinarily be used in prose but are not fully necessary for understanding (a technique intermittently used throughout the book).

Audio recording of Storni's reading this poem on PV.

6 OP starts the line "las ola! [sic] de las nubes," which I have corrected as a misprint (VD has the line as shown here).

8 "Turning blue" would have had the wrong connotations.

10 "Carro" can refer to the carriage of a typewriter as well as the more usual "cart" or "car."

13 DRAE says "lunado" means "crescent-shaped" though here it seems to be almost a past participle of the non-existent verb "lunar," i.e. "moonlit" or "half-moonlit" ("lit by a half-moon," not "half lit by the moon").

The River Plate, Mist-Silvered in Celestial Blue

"Sky blue" (instead of "celestial blue") would too closely repeat the "sky" of the first line of the poem. The poem seems to revolve around the idea of blurring the horizon (which at times functions as a mirror) between above and below, air and water. With varying degrees of success, it deploys paired sentence structures (with doubled words embedded) that also embody this main idea.

4 Forms like "tiéndese" seem poetic, meant to evoke archaic or Iberian Spanish. See B&B, 11.14.1 note ii.

"Llanura" is used in the next poem, "The River Plate in Rain," as well. Here I translate it "plains," a metaphor for the horizon as the sky, personified, lies down on it. The final stanza of "The River Plate in Rain" uses "llanura" in the context of a more abstract description of what might be called a spiritual state, so I translate it as "flatness."

5-8   There is elegance and parallelism in this stanza that I am afraid does not come through in English.

6   "Filo" is used in a different sense in the poem after next, "Ravines of the River Plate in Colonia."

6-7   "Comba" and "copo" are both problematic. "Comba" could be "the curvature of the earth" or the "curve of a valley of water created by swells in the sea" (as I have chosen to interpret it); but it could also have something to do with the curve of a sail (not to mention "warp," "sag," "jump rope" or "tree root"). "Copo" usually means a "flake or ball of something soft" but can also mean "a clot," "a type of fishing net" or "a treetop" in addition to a sense used in the Southern Cone ("piled-up clouds") that I have chosen here.

7   I use "navigated" to avoid "sailed" as "sail" is not exactly repeated in the original ("vela" then "navegaba").

13-14 Unclear what distinction is being made.

The River Plate in Rain

This poem uses "literary imperfect" throughout.

1   ORM has "almost squeezed you."

4   English-Spanish dictionaries list "pyx" for "copón," but the DRAE definition more closely describes photos of "ciborium" found online.

9   "A plomo" means "true/vertical/plumb" but here is part of the set phrase "caer a plomo" ("to fall flat"). ORM's "pounded like lead" captures this sense as well.

11   ORM has the crosses "turned slovenly."

13   The verb "dormir" ("sleep") is usually intransitive, and it is unclear whether "sueño" is meant to be "sleep" or "dream." "Dream" would normally take the verb "soñar," ("dream"), so I (unlike ORM) have gone with "sleep."

14   See note on "llanura" above ("The River Plate, Mist-Silvered in Celestial Blue," line four).

Ravines of the River Plate in Colonia

In an audio recording (see PV) Storni says that she wrote this poem upon arriving in Uruguay one afternoon and that it is "an impression between subjective and objective of that landscape."

1   In the audio recording, this sounds like "redobles verdes de tambor los sapos," a more natural phrasing to my ears.

8   See note on line six of "The River Plate, Mist-Silvered in Celestial Blue."

12   "Morados" could also be "bruises." "Rompe dique" with no article before "dique" almost suggests that the dam breaks the sky rather than the reverse.

Colonia at Midnight

10-11 Note displacement of "de las aves" from "canto" that would sound highly unnatural in speech.

Big Buenos Aires Dance

Danzón is a particular dance and genre of music, originating in Cuba in 1879, that incorporates European precedents along with African and indigenous elements. By line seven, where it is explicitly mentioned (if not earlier), the reader realizes that the title refers, by way of analogy, to the Argentine tango. Or perhaps the analogy is really between the tango and the dirty but coordinated industrial activities of the city. In this case "danzón" could be translated (as I have done) as a generic "danza" ("dance") with an augmentative suffix. The tango for Storni is thus de-romanticized and disembodied.

1-8   ORM prudently separates the first stanza into two sentences, but I think the original wording is still clear and deliberately sets up the strong image of line five ("vi plegarse tu negro Puente Alsina"), around which the second stanza is unified.

4   "Tramonto" is an Italian word for sunset, twilight or, figuratively, decline/waning.

8   Unclear whether this is "a las barcazas" as in "vi a las barcazas." Do the barges take an *a personal* because they are "dancing"? It is also possible that "a las barcazas" means "at the barges," and the dancers are the waters, cellars and factories that follow the colon at the end of this line.

13   OP has "pethos devorados," but it seems safe to call this a misprint as ORM and VD have "pechos." "Pechos" could also be lungs or hearts.

The Furies of Buenos Aires

C&B (page 190) gives a translation of the final stanza of this poem after explaining that, in M&T, "the cityscape acquires force for its starkness and alienation," leading to "a terrifying sense of the grotesque" that is here "coarsely presented."

5   "Alzan" could be "they raise," but Storni does sometimes seem to use "alzar" in the sense of "alzarse con" ("to run off with"). This is perhaps equivalent to using "lift" informally to mean "steal" in English. Other connotations of "alzar" include hiding and clearing away. The walls could also be simply "thick" or the remains of a ruined building, in which case "señales" could be "street signs."

8   "Verdín" could be "scum/green slime," but this stanza seems to occur out of the water. "Se esperezan" is a form of "se desperezan" ("they stir their limbs").

12   C&B has "lid" for "chapa."

13   C&B has "beady eyes" for "ojos grises."

American Sun

Unclear whether this is literary boosterism – as in an awakening to the New World's poetic possibilities (with a pert parenthetical dismissal of male writers) – or a claim for the New World's aridity, to be escaped only in dreams of (or poems about) the sea.

7   "Limo blando" ("soft muck") appears again in the next poem, "Suggestion of a Willow." "Holgada" could also be "roomy" or "baggy," but "comfortable" includes its other sense: "well-to-do."

10   Puzzling placement of "minúscula" ("miniscule" or "lower case"), which I suppose could also refer to "mirilla" ("peephole"). It seems to me that the speaker is waking up here and is awake for the final stanza.

12   "Su" ("its") in this line and in line fourteen could refer to a few different antecedents but all to similar effect.

Suggestion of a Willow

The "suggestion" of the somewhat hackneyed image of a weeping willow next to a pond for Storni is actually a macabre inversion of the title that is anything but the expected pastoral. The reader is invited to witness a slimy netherworld (under the pond's surface?) where up and down are confused.

1-2   Since there is no strong rhyme in the original, I avoided "city of moss" with "cross."

3-4   Perhaps these angels represent dragonflies as seen from under water.

5-8   This stanza's grammar, seemingly straining to capture the special miasma, is difficult to parse: see the distance, reminiscent of the Spanish Baroque, between the noun "viudas" ("widows," with the connotation of "ghosts" in Argentina, or even "black widow spiders") and its modifier "balanceadas" (difficult to say whether "swaying" or "balanced" is the right sense of the word). One would expect, perhaps, the yellowish wind-widows to blur the glass, but the singular verb "desdibuja" indicates that they (swaying weeping-willow branches?) are the objects of action by the glass (water's surface?) in the inverted world.

7   OP and VD have "amarillos," but the masculine plural makes little sense: a modifier for "espejos" ("mirrors") at the end of the line would be extremely odd even in this context. I have therefore used "amarilloso" ("yellowish," modifying "viento"/"wind"). This has the advantage of clearer expression and achieves a more natural-sounding eleven-syllable line if substituted in the original Spanish. In the OP/VD version, an eleventh syllable must be produced via hiatus (suspension of synaloepha) between "viento" and "amarillos." Storni bends many rules but in this book never varies the traditionally-counted hendecasyllable.

9   "Stitch" could be "dot," "period" or any of several other senses.

11   "Clover" could be "clubs" (as in the suit of cards), but the only other instance of "trébol" in M&T, apart from the title of the book, is in "Ball in the Water," where it also seems to refer to the common plant.

Locusts

Perhaps there is a military analogy here, which would not be surprising given the German and Japanese invasions of 1938: a locust is not "made" for intentional destructive action just an airplane usually is not; but both did and do destroy, especially in groups, "distributed harmoniously" (in formation?) in the sky. Storni probably drew on knowledge of World War I for this poem, but it presages the larger-scale air raids of World War II (and perhaps even twenty-first-century drone strikes). As the poem goes on, "y" takes over from "para" as the repeated drumbeat. The overall effect seems to me both clumsy and chilling. My translation is fairly literal (see line three) in order to retain both tendencies as well as the formal parallelism.

5	In 1938, more people had probably seen an autogiro, introduced in 1923, than a helicopter, first flown in 1936. But a contemporary readership is unlikely to know the word "autogiro," and if shown a picture of one, would probably call it a "helicopter" (or perhaps "little helicopter"). Since the English word "helicopter" dates to the late nineteenth century, it should not be an anachronism here.

The Sunflower

The first three stanzas start with a past-tense verb ("before here"), but the fourth switches to present, with the speaker again "here" in her garden examining a "real" sunflower.
8	This wording elides the possessive pronoun and thus the question of whether the "farolas" belong to the sunflower or to the sun, but the line is still awkward in English.
9	"Lanzas" could be purse-snatchers or thieves in Argentina.
10	The sunflower seems to be the one falling, but the lances could be as well. The lack of a comma at the end of line nine inserts a small doubt.
11	A 1930 Spanish newspaper article (*A B C*, 21 February 1930) uses "alzarse en frase" in the sense of rising up ready with a phrase to strike. This goes along with the lances and the "blow" of wine. However, "alzarse" sometimes means "to abscond with," going along with the "thief" meaning above. Perhaps the sunflower (head) is having trouble formulating a retort to his own abdomen (lines seven and eight)?
14	This seems to be an epithet for the sunflower, but it might also refer to the speaker.

Plea to Prometheus

This kind of speaker – high-toned, issuing commands in spirited and eloquent defiance – is a specialty and a strength of Storni's.
2	There is a cluster of tooth-related words here: the millstone could also be a molar tooth but itself has "teeth" (grooves?) like a cog in a watch.
4	Not clear whether "ella" is "tu roca" or "la muela" (or even "la noche"). "Rodar" supports the interpretation of "muela" as "millstone" rather than "molar" in line two.
12	Unlike the prior three, this stanza does not start with a command. "He aquí a" could be rendered, as in the Bible, "behold," but I thought that would be over the top here. The action is finally frozen into a strong metaphorical image of the Promethean woman.

The Son

Until its last stanza, this poem seems to suppress most definite and indefinite articles, with an effect of compression that is difficult to reproduce in English.

1-2 "Estás ciega para ampararlo" is not clear to me but seems to convey caring for a fetus that of course nobody can see directly – or simply not knowing how to care for an infant.

3 Odd phrasing for "not knowing whether it's a boy or a girl." The comma at the end of this line does seem to indicate that "por flores de mujer o espadas de hombre" is not an adverbial phrase modifying "ignoras." It is rather the first of three (negatively formulated) noun phrases, which are objects of "ignoras." I use "cannot tell" here to differentiate "ignoras" from "no sabes si" in line thirteen.

5 This line could begin "Swaying back and forth, you rock him," but I was unsure about the idea that "you," while rocking your son, are also rocking back and forth (like a ship?). "Vacillating" while rocking also describes a double motion and serves to foreshadow the darker tone of the rest of the poem. Unclear whether "branch of air" identifies "you" or "your son."

9 "Apenas," more ambiguously, could be "only."

12 Perhaps "frase" ("phrase") is meant to be "fase" ("phase").

13 Note the more general "el que empuja," ("that which pushes"), not "él que empuja" ("he who pushes").

14 I hesitantly think "sierpe" must be the direct object of "arrolla" (with "el que empuja" as the subject). However, "desplegarse" is not transitive, so the angel must unfold itself.

Suggestion of an Empty Crib

The suggestion could be a ghost or an influence. Despite the title, the crib does not stay empty past the first stanza.

4 "Rosa" should not take a personal "a," so it seems to be the object of a preposition (which could also be rendered "in").

9 "Franjas" could also be "fringes."

10 "Him" could be "it" (the little frog) or "it" (the crib).

12 Passive voice as "acunar" does not seem to have a reflexive form. Again, "he" could be "it."

Time of Sterility

This poem seems to depict a woman's transition from menstruation and fertility to menopause through a series of mythic images. The "numbers" seem to represent mortal time in the form of cycles that eventually come to an end. Perhaps the "lukewarm faces" in the third stanza are the Woman's children as their maturation would certainly presage or coincide with the "time of sterility."

4-8   ORM uses "their" and "them," perhaps interpreting "sus" as "belonging to the numbers."

8   "Ordenaba" could also be "ordained" (as in ORM), but I think the Christian overtone a bit out of place here.

9   Possessives throughout the poem ("sus" again in this line) can be read as either "the river's" or "the Woman's."

12   "Seno" would more commonly mean "breast," but here an alternate, figurative sense seemed to work better.

Baroque Self-Portrait

The middle stanzas of this poem contain a sequence of neutral images, in contrast to the concern for the grotesque indulged in the first and final stanzas. This structure may reflect the idea of life sandwiched between historical non-existence and a late period of illness and death, though the latter assumes the position of the former for the next generation (as illustrated by the example of the Greeks).

The title indicates that the poem is dedicated to self-description – or that the speaker is describing a painting of herself. Taking my cue from "mi calzante cara" in line three and "me dobló el pecho" in line twelve, I take any parts of the body in this poem to belong to the speaker (those that are preceded by definite articles at least).

3   "Calzante," though obviously related to "calzar," seems not to be a recognized word in Spanish. Perhaps it is borrowed from Italian ("fitting," "appropriate," or "shoehorn"). ORM's "fastened to my face, taut as leather" creatively brings out the right connotations. My version's rhyme of "space" and "face" is a little sing-song, but the original also has strong sound echoes.

5-6   ORM has "blew tropical / gusts from the south," but to me the language here seems more heightened than that.

6-7 "Broke open its suns / on my head" follows the pattern of the mask's falling onto the speaker's head, and, later, the freezing of sounds against the speaker's skull. "Cut open its suns / over my head [contents spilling out]" is also possible. ORM has "releasing suns / to shine on the head."

8 The speaker has exchanged her living, organic acanthus wreath (or crown) for the dead, inorganic metal hair of a statue. Note the myth of Acantha, who, in refusing Apollo's advances, scratched his face. He then turned her into the thorny plant acanthus as punishment.

9 ORM's "moonstone" again creatively finds the right connotations.

9-10 Unclear why (aside from syllable count) not "tan ligero / que lo acunaban las rosas."

11-12 Alluding to Storni's breast cancer?

12 The sounds seem to emanate from "the organ" but could be distantly associated with any of the subjects of the preceding sentences.

Youths

"Youths" here is meant either abstractly ("concepts of youth") or in the sense of "periods of youthfulness as experienced or remembered by one or more persons," and not to refer to a group of young people, which would be "jóvenes." Storni proves characteristically contrarian in this racy poem that casts the speaker's long-buried "youths" as grotesque if morbidly beautiful and intense.

1 The repeated instances of "they" and "them," though clunky, I found unavoidable in English.

2-4 I felt obliged to make it clear that the youths – and not the poem's speaker – are watchful.

6 "Abridoras" recalls "abrideras," which describes fruit that is easily removed from its rind. "Capullo" here could even be read as "glans/prepuce" (see line eleven).

7 I chose "bore" to go along with the fruit/vegetation motif.

11 "De-tasseled" like an ear of corn perhaps.

13 "Reverdecido" (as in vegetation that has become green again) is part of a geological/agricultural motif, so I didn't want to leave it at "revived air."

Forces

    1   "Espada" can mean swordsman or matador, but that would have to be "ese espada." Here it does not seem to refer to the suit of cards, "spades," though that would compliment "trébol" ("clubs") in the book's title. In Argentina, "espada" can mean a lock pick (ordinarily "ganzúa") according to DRAE.

    8   "El abra" could be a measure of the width of a sailing ship's rigging.

    9   The repeated "there" for "allá" has a heavy effect. "Steer" here in the nautical sense (common throughout M&T).

    10   "Aspa" is sometimes used in Argentina to mean "asta" ("bull's horn"), echoing the bullfighting connotations elsewhere in the poem. Here it also seems to include alternate meanings like "windmill sail," "x-shape/cross" and "mechanical reel (for winding)."

    13   "Alfanje" can also mean "swordfish," alluding to the opening line of this poem.

    14   "Florecer" is not usually transitive.

Return to Sanity

"Cordura" could also be translated as "sense," as in "I returned to my senses," or even "prudence/wisdom," throughout. "Regreso" could also mean "I return." The poem seems to be spoken by a mythic god and addressed to another mythic god, both having significant power over nature.

    3   I interpret "árbol" as "mast" rather than "tree" given the nautical images that proliferate here.

    4   "Casa de luz" is not the normal way to say "lighthouse" in Spanish, but it may apply in this line.

    11   This line strikes me as a little wry, which is why I used the slightly unnatural "very sanely." "Lo" ("it") could refer to "tu amor" ("your love") or to "el borde de la Sombra" ("the edge of Shadow"), but these are both used objects of prepositions, not normally antecedents for an object pronoun. "The sea" is a more likely candidate for "it" as is more plain in line seven. This also makes sense in the narrative: "you" perform an action on the sun (first stanza) and another act on the sea (second stanza), and then "I" stitch the two together. Nevertheless, the distance between any mention of the sea and "lo" injects ambiguity, which I tried to keep by not rearranging the stanza's lines to point to the sea's being joined with the sun.

12   This last stanza quickens the pace with visibly shorter words. What is "fixed in place"? Most likely "the sea," though "your love" and the speaker's sanity are also possibilities.

13-14 Ambiguity multiplies. "Se reajusta al mar" would make it more clear that the flock is adjusting to the sea rather than "the flock adjusts the sea." A freer translation would probably opt to read "al" as "el": "and warned, / the enraged sea adjusts its flock [of waves]." "Avisado" could also mean "sensible."

Base of a Tree

Audio recording of Storni's reading this poem on PV.

"Pie de árbol" these days can mean "Christmas-tree skirt" though that is clearly not the sense intended in this poem, a terrifying vision personal and collective calamity, the victims and perpetrators of which can be assigned identities by the reader.

11   "Detained" is quite literal, but "we stopped" makes one wonder, "stopped what?" "Hid" or "huddled" would be more sentimental than, and not really implied by, "detenerse."

Return to My Birds

The birds and mirrored city invite interpretation as symbols, perhaps referring to aspects of poetry itself.

3   MF has "under its streetlights."

5   "Ronda" here is suggestive: as a noun it could mean a group of musicians in the streets at night, a ring road, or a street in an old walled city (or a round of negotiations, cards, beverages, etc.). It is also possible to take the phrase "en ronda" (arranged in a circle, especially people) as modifying "voces": "And in their [or its] lofty ring were great voices."

6   "Pompal" seems to be a Storni coinage, so I use "pomp" as an adjective even though it's normally a noun in English.

7   "Papered" could also be "wallpapered," "papered-over" or "paper-lined."

8   I wanted to keep the unusual adjective placement.

10   OP and VD have a period at the end of this line (curious as the next line is not capitalized), but I have removed it as it seems to be an inconsequential mistake. A comma instead is also possible.

12   One wonders how the speaker frees herself.

14   The question may refer to Jesus's cry from the cross, i.e. "Why hast thou forsaken me?" The period at the end this line (following a question mark and closing quotation marks) seemed within the realm of possibility for historical Spanish punctuation, but I have not allowed it in English.

The Siren

3   Note that September is springtime in Argentina.

7-8   ORM has "bread of life," but "vida" could also be a term of endearment. I see "vida" as the addressee of the preceding list of commands.

9   Does the machine produce various shades of blue, or is the machine painted in various blue colors, or is the machine itself made of blue colors?

10   Ambiguous as to whether the speaker is saying to leave her the blues machine and one vivid thought, or to leave her the blues machine and that the blues machine releases pulleys and a thought (though the former seems more likely). Recall that sex is buried among pulleys in the opening poem "To Eros."

12   "Alentar" seems to be intransitive here, so I have not translated it as "to encourage." "Lo" and "él" here seem to be the "vivid thought" from line eleven.

Trite Words for the Moon

6   Both OP and VD have "amé" ("I loved") instead of "aymé," (meaning "ay de mí," a sigh), but that would place the speaker "on" the river and lead to an abrupt transition back to addressing "you," the moon. With "aymé" (as is used in versions found online), the whole stanza can be taken as pure description of the river and then the moon (i.e. "you"), interrupted only by a sigh from the speaker (but with no real verb).

Grand Painting

The title phrase can also mean "the big picture" (i.e. the greater context) though I do not know when or how widely this usage spread.

The speaker first distances herself from what she describes ("aquellas ruinas," "allí") but then in the last two lines enters the rather somber scene described in the poem – just as the reader enters the poem itself from "outside the frame" of the "grand painting." Storni sets up an implied equivalence between the willing "surrender" of a reader or viewer of art to the work and, on the other hand, the act of dying. Death, slyly imagined as a medieval painter of Christian allegory at its most humorless, occupies the same position as the poet, who plays with the idea of a static conceit somewhat facetiously.

8 Borges used the phrase "cielo amanzanado" more approvingly years earlier in an elegy to Buenos Aires: "Elegía de Palermo" ("Elegy of Palermo"), written and published in the magazine *Nosotros* in 1926 and included under the title "Elegía de los portones" ("Elegy of the Gates") in Borges's 1929 poetry collection *Cuaderno San Martín* (*San Martín Notebook*).

9 DLM (page 235) has "un cuervo herido" and "a wounded crow" instead of "ciervo herido" ("wounded deer" with "stag" implied by the antlers).

Ultratelephone

I take the first two stanzas as quoted dialogue over "ultratelephone" from this life to the afterlife (as in ORM's English title, "Phone Call to the Afterlife"). The speaker first asks for Horacio and then addresses him, apparently without hearing a reply. (Horacio is presumed to be Storni's friend, the well-known Argentine writer Horacio Quiroga, who killed himself while suffering from cancer in 1937, a year before Alfonsina Storni would do the same.) A similar pattern is followed with the speaker's father in the second stanza. In the final two stanzas, both men are addressed – though the statements are no longer presented as dialogue in quotation marks. It is as though the speaker has hung up the ultratelephone and reverted to her standard poetic voice, which fades to that of pure narrator in the final stanza. Appropriately for Quiroga, she sketches a small incident with a touch of the horror, which trails off into tenderness and melancholy.

5 MF has "flask" for "damajuana" while ORM has "demijohn." A cursory online image search for "damajuana" showed what I immediately thought of as "(glass) wine jugs," so I decided to use this less obscure term.

11 MF sees a collective killing of the toad.

12 MF and ORM have the toad as the subject of "miraba," but the idea that the toad watched itself being finished off by the cousins is odd to me.

14 I wanted to highlight the imperfect tense of "seguían" by keeping the phrase set off by a semicolon. ORM has an elegant solution in "and roses formed a cortege." However, I take the tone as less formal, and the word "cortejo" ("cortege") does not appear.

Ball in the Water

    7   "Crespo" here could mean curly-edged or something more abstract like "in a tortuous style."
    10   The original line does have quite a few "o" sounds, but "the low sky and a slow lowing" would be too much.

Cicada on a Moonlit Night

    Audio recording of Storni's reading this poem on PV.
    5   ORM has a different interpretation here ("sobre" is "against," and the toads are the enemy of the crickets), which may very well be correct.
    10   "Muy de azules" seems to describe a person who favors the color blue, but just "very blue" is also possible.

Flower in a Hand

    Audio recording of Storni's reading this poem on PV, partially translated in DLM.
    4   The subject position in this stanza shifts from the hand to the flower.
    10   "Boneless" would have false overtones of store-bought meat.
    11   Here I include both English senses of the word "entregada" as each seems equally present and appropriate.
    13   This seems to me a reference to the Book of Revelation; but "lacres" could just as easily mean "Satanic reds," so I include that sense as well. Perhaps these combinations are clumsy, but in each pair of senses both do come through in the poem I think – important to convey given the duality of the hand/flower.
    14   "Artes negras sabedoras" seems to be a phrase unique to Storni, so I try not to turn it into a cliché.

One of the Women

Variations on "Any Woman," "Some Woman" and "A Woman" for the title all seemed to strike the wrong tone in English while "One of the Women" I hope balances the indeterminacy of "alguna" with the ironic intent I detect: as if the speaker's attitude were "the woman to be described, whose intentions may not be benign, is singularly impressive, but then again so is just about any woman you might see on the street." The meaning of "Biblia" – beyond the literal – escapes me. Calle Florida is a central pedestrian shopping street in Buenos Aires.

1   The "Azogue" could be a ship, referring to the historical transport of mercury needed to refine precious metals in Peru and Mexico. Perhaps the woman is arriving in Buenos Aires from Europe (or returning home from Europe, as Storni did a couple times).

4   "Filtrando" could also be "leaking." It's not clear whether the "asp greens" come from the woman's face and are filtered by the threads of night – or are the threads of night emitting the "asp greens"? "Tramado" often implies a "plot" or "plan to deceive."

12   I assume that "en rojo labio" refers to the woman.

13   "Composes" in the sense of "to compose/write," "to fix/mend," "to settle/soothe" and even "to make up/be the constituent parts of."

14   "Arrolla" could mean "winds up" or "rolls up" (this sense seems to be used in "Mar de pantalla").

Planes in a Twilight

1   "Azúrea" could refer to the Latin name of a flowering plant commonly called "bugloss," but I have taken it to be made up by Storni as something approximating "azure."

Cloud Zoo

2   "Osito" could be "teddy bear" (as in ORM). "Señora" likewise could be "mistress."

4   The use of a comma here and another in line six seem pleasingly odd in Spanish. The effect partially comes through in English.

7-9   Perhaps a real crane (rather than a crane-shaped cloud) flies through the belly of the cloud-whale and out where the eye would be.

11   "Escándalos alzaba" is a phrasing apparently unique to Storni.

Airplane in a Mirror

In the second stanza, the speaker seems to be *in* the airplane, perhaps presaging Julio Cortázar's "La isla a mediodía" ("The Island at Noon") from 1966.

2   "Through" here could mean either "through space" or "by the agency of." For "mal de ensueño," I take DRAE's definition of "de ensueño": "Ideal, fantástico, maravilloso."

14   "Asomar" has the connotation of "showing through an aperture" or "sticking out," ideas that unfortunately don't fully carry through to English equivalents.

Nest in a Statue

1   "Recogido" could also be "retiring" or "modest."

5   "Malva" (also used for "mauve" in Spanish) I think refers to a flowering plant that climbs the statue, further characterized (almost tenderly) as fitting into a heraldic design.

10   I find it difficult to interpret "por lecho" here.

11   Smiled at the boy? Or at the wretch?

12   In whom? The boy or the wretch? The nest?

13   "Como distante" and "como invisible" are lovely but hard to parse. As distant/invisible as the two rivers?

The Sky

As often occurs in M&T, it seems to be both night and day in this poem.

4   "Bitten" and "burned" are also possible for "picados."

9   OP begins this line "¡Ay!, qué poeta," but then line fourteen would end with an unpaired exclamation point. Therefore I have used "¡Ay, qué poeta" as in VD.

10   Not entirely clear whether the poet or the torrent could "give me the sky."

13   Since "antorcha" is singular and seems to belong to all the children, "torch" seems less likely than "guide" (perhaps the poet – or the sun).

14   ORM reads "jugar a no toparse" as "hide-and-seek."

The Fleeing Cadaver

This one is remarkable in its willingness to push the grotesque and macabre. The rhythm's stops and starts contribute to this quality. The positioning of adjectives before the nouns they modify ("yacente losa," "nacida noche," "animales olas") throws things gently off-kilter as well.

2   "Se yergue," here interpreted as reflexive, could also be passive-voice though the effect would change little. "Losa" could be "tombstone."

5   Or it may be that the fibers cut time into the hours. However, I like the phrasing chosen because it contains the idea that the dead and dying mourn as well: they mourn time's demise. For them Storni suggests the terrifying feeling of a taut wire's (or muscle's) being cut and going slack.

7   "Nacida noche" could mean the risen night sky as well.

13   Could the cadaver be rolling downhill to hell, trying to keep cool? Perhaps "sus neveras" ("his iceboxes") was meant to be singular.

Siren of a Ship in Port

At first I found this dramatization of trauma and violence baffling but now would offer an example of a possible reading, though there is sufficient ambiguity to admit others: one might imagine that the speaker in this poem addresses a sailor from a whaling ship who had been knocked overboard – either by a harpooned whale's hitting the ship or by the "other fish," seemingly magical and perhaps from a submarine blue city. Then again the events of the third stanza could have occurred later, perhaps that night. At any rate, the sailor descended to the city below, was mistreated, escaped, surfaced on dry land and is now trying to explain what happened. The twist is that the speaker somehow already knows the whole story and is, by way of interrupting the protagonist, the one telling it. Perhaps this is meant to evoke the uncanny, or perhaps it's just a playful bit of rhetoric.

Alternatively, the addressee could be the boat itself, or even three or four separate sailors (each given a stanza or two) who experienced the siren while at sea.

1   This can't be "you were floating" as second person is already marked as informal with "no grites." However, it is not clear whether the subject of "estaba" is the boat or the siren. "Boyar" does contain the sense of a boat's return to the water after being stored on dry land.

3   "Lo" must be the dog as the siren would be "la."

10   "Alone" here is masculine, meaning the siren is not being addressed as "you."

11   "Knocked over" could be "knocked around."

12   This could be just "they cut your arms."

Suggestion of Birdsong

This poem doesn't possess the consistent mood and strong forward motion of many others in the collection.

4   "Enciende" here seems to have been made intransitive, but even "se enciende" ("lights up," "turns on," "catches fire") is odd when the subject is the immortal spirit of Socrates.

5   "El dedo de la envidia" seems to be a set phrase related to the idea that the act of pointing at and/or finding fault with someone is an indication of secret jealousy.

10   This seems to be a variant on the expression for "biting at heels": "morder los talones."

Sleep

Storni really declaimed her poems when reciting (see notes on "Barrancas del Plata en Colonia"). In "Sleep," the cadence strikes me as formal as well, so I have attempted something analogous for the English version.

ORM renders the title "The Dream," but "Sleep" edges closer to the connotation of death apparent throughout the poem.

1-2   These lines are ambiguously worded and could be read as "A lukewarm mask falls from another, icy one over your face." The words seem to be arranged to maximize the effect of "sobre tu cara cae" as the culmination of the assonance in the first line.

ORM has a slightly different take though also rearranging the words to preserve the alliteration of "cara cae" as "face falls."

1-4   Note that the first stanza contains no punctuation while semicolons break up the second.

4   ORM has "the flower droops." Perhaps the idea is that flowers wilt as time flies. In my version "la flor" means flowers generally, and they flee the misty landscape.

6   "Enflorar" seems to be a rare word meaning "to adorn with flowers." Perhaps Storni meant it as "to blossom" ("florecer") given that the semicolons at the end of line five and after "sospecha" seem to indicate that "mito" is not the subject of the verb "enflora," which is therefore intransitive.

7   Perhaps there is a semicolon missing before "y el iris luce."

9-10   ORM has "The state of being is greater than nonbeing" and renders "doblado, / prendido" as "bent, clutching." In contrast I think "doblado" here refers to the doubled self: the person sleeping ("un ser") and the disembodied person as projected in his dream ("un no ser"/"un más ser") – the person caught in reality and the physically "absent" dream consciousness. "Doblado" can even mean "dubbed" (an apt analogy: in dreaming we are dubbed into a dream language).

12   "Alentador" and "sagaz" are both adjectives, but I have to treat one of them as a noun here and have chosen "sagaz." ORM has "alentador" (translated "encouragement" rather than "encourager") as the noun.

God-Force

1   "Arquitectar" seems to be a Storni neologism.
2-3   Note how "cruza" is inserted in the middle of "el paso de Jehová fuerte."
5   "Echar a nacer" is an unusual expression.
7   "Descolorantes" is a variant of "decolorantes."
9   Perhaps there is a comma or semicolon missing at the end of this line.

Allegory of Spring

The poem may be inspired by two famous Botticelli paintings, *Allegory of Spring* and *The Birth of Venus*. The second of these features, on the upper left, a female zephyr with her hand on a male companion's waist – and indeed something similar occurs in the final stanza of "Allegory of Spring."

Storni seems to be experimenting here by mixing pastoral conventions with the grotesque. Except for the second stanza, which uses innocent tropes in the first two lines before shading into a sinister undertone for the third and fourth, the images all seem deliberately ugly. The conclusion, that the rejuvenation of springtime is a dream or illusion in which we drown, is therefore one of Storni's most brutal.

At the risk of forcing some inelegant wording, I wanted to keep the strong pattern of starting lines with "and."

1   It is unclear whether spring is searching for the earth, or earth is searching for spring. However, spring personified seems to be the subject of the poem.
2   "Yermar" is usually transitive but here seems to have no object.

7   "Pomo" could have alternate meanings as discussed elsewhere. "Cajas" could mean "coffins."

9   This line is unclear to me, especially the meaning of "fila." DRAE defines "torzón" as a shortened form of "torozón," meaning an animal with colic (and/or its movements), but "torozón" can also mean "unease" in general. Perhaps "torzones fila" should read "torzones en fila." If "torzones" were the subject, the verb would be "desgreñan." "Fila" can also mean "antipathy" or "animosity" in the expression "tener fila a alguién." So if "fila" were the subject, we would have "Animosity dishevels the sky's agonies."

11   "Los" has to be "torzones."

12   "El hombre" here I take to mean man in the abstract as otherwise, with no precedent, "un hombre" would be more appropriate.

13   Possibly "her chest."

14   I have attempted to provide an approximation of the unusual phrasing "largas sus trompetas" ("sus trompetas largas" would be more expected). Fantasy or even man could also be the trumpets' owner.

Screen Ocean

I do not translate the title as "On-Screen Ocean" because that would have to be "Mar en la pantalla," as in the second line of the poem, not "Mar de pantalla."

The final line of this poem is repeated as the first line of its sequel, "Animated Drawings," where the mystical flower is the source of color for artistic creation. In "Mar de pantalla," the origin of the flower is described in terms of the sea (a frequent theme in M&T), or rather, the experience of watching the sea in a movie, or one's memory of the sea as filtered through all five senses. Perhaps the progression from "Screen Ocean" to "Animated Drawings" is one from consumer to producer of art (with a synthesis of the two toward the end of the second poem).

1   Punctuation is omitted throughout this stanza as in the original, and the repetitious *and*s are kept.

8   This line is not entirely clear to me. "Goce" could mean "enjoyment" either in the sense of pleasure or in the sense of possession.

9   There may be a comparison here between the action at a distance of a movie projector on the screen and the moon's influence on the sea (i.e. tides) – and, for that matter, the on-screen image's action at a distance on the audience. Perhaps "máquinas" means "stage machinery."

12   This clause could be reversed to read "The sea that coils the celluloid escapes." "Arrollar" here could also be "to wash/sweep away," as in "The sea that sweeps away the celluloid escapes."

Animated Drawings

The third and fourth stanzas of this poem develop the theme of the first two – the history of human creativity – by sweetly focusing on a character in an animated movie and by addressing the reader directly. Both techniques show a sympathy unusual for Storni.

1-4 Note the repetition of the last line of the previous poem.

1 I have tried to replicate the placement of the subject at the very beginning ("una mística flor"), followed by a series of appositives, and the verb ("viene") at the very end of the sentence.

2 "Pomo" here could have several meanings: round handle, flask, tube (as in a tube of paint) or a toy container used to throw water during carnival. Therefore I have used an ambiguous term, "reservoir," as well.

5-8 "Desentrañar" here could also mean "to figure out" or "to unravel the mystery of." Except that the last part of the sentence ("hasta lograr un árbol que camina") indicates an ongoing action, I would have translated the first three lines of this stanza as "It has been millions of years since man's audacious claw, by gutting it [the flower], painted walls and bit the stones." I think the implication is that animated movies (including one in which a tree comes to life and walks) are the simply the latest form of cave painting.

9 Perhaps this refers to Mickey Mouse (who debuted in one of the first sound cartoons in 1928). Storni was involved in children's theater and wrote characters from well-known stories into her plays.

12-14 Here again there is some suggestion of the first official Mickey Mouse cartoon, *Steamboat Willie*. Incidentally, at one point in *Steamboat Willie*, a goat chews on a few pages of sheet music (labeled "Turkey in the Straw, Hey! Hey!"). The note markings then drop from its mouth (and are heard sounding as they hit the floor) as if they could leave the page as objects – an idea that is explored in the next poem.

Musical Page

Telephone poles, which one imagines hold up the wire "staves" described in this poem, appear prominently in another 1928 Mickey Mouse animation called *Plane Crazy* (see notes for lines nine to fourteen of "Animated Drawings" above).

1 "It" is the sheet of music, though this is more clear in Spanish given the pronoun "la." "Tramonto" is an Italian word, perhaps in use in Argentina. The meaning changes slightly if "al" is understood as "to the," as in "I saw it written to the sunset, indecipherable."

6   If the papyrus is to be construed as a plant rather than a surface to write on, "on" should be changed to "in."

9   This stanza structures the poem by providing a momentary lull before nightfall (though one bird/note remains on the wires or aloft). Otherwise the extended metaphor would be too static.

10   "Al pronto" seems oddly placed here, and I am unsure exactly how to render this line.

11   That the stave is silenced and yet a note remains could be a contradiction or an attempt at eeriness. Perhaps the birds have been replaced with bats in the next stanza.

12   "Crotchets and quavers" would be shorter, but I prefer the American "quarter notes and eighth notes" (not "quarter and eighth notes," which implies a jumble of both where I think the text implies one after the other, i.e. a quickening of tempo).

14   "Reajustar" here seems to come from "ajustar" in the typographical sense. "Plana" could be "page in a newspaper" as well as the plain observed in the poem.

An Ear

1   The first three stanzas form a long apostrophe to the titular ear.

2   DLM uses "grooves" for "estrías," but I think "fluting" works for grooves in ivory.

3   "Valva" (used for "half shell," especially in Argentina) is like a singular form of bivalve, not the generic "válvula" used for mechanical water and air valves.

5   DLM has "rosy," but "roseate" echoes the zoological tone of "valva."

7   "Punzada" does not refer to an ear pierced for earrings as "to pierce one's ear" is "perforarse la oreja." Perhaps the meaning here is "shot through with enveloping labyrinths."

10   It's clear in Spanish that "dibujada" and "hecha" refer to the ear, so I have re-arranged the phrasing in English in an attempt to make this clear.

13   Storni poetically leaves out "is," as in the more prosaic "there deep inside, black is the underground where the lion of thought roars." I repeat Storni's omission for a somewhat old-fashioned effect in English.

A Pencil

Unusually for this volume, "A Pencil" mostly deals with scenes from everyday urban reality, and the third stanza's list of purse contents is Storni at her most down-to-earth. Also unusual are the implication that the speaker is a writer and the frequency of concrete, first-person verbs in the past tense — as though the speaker were an independent woman like Storni. However, the notion of a pencil as a concealed explosive comes across as an awkwardly ominous update of the old comparison between the pen and the sword — and leads to a curious form of literary bragging in this poem as if to say "I can terrorize the world with only my words."

In the translation I have added a few commas that are not necessary in Spanish but help in English. However, the last stanza conveys acceleration, surprise and confusion; so I omit a comma that one might put after "don't know where."

2   Here and in line six, the verb is fused with its object pronoun (which strikes me as slightly archaic) even though this does not seem necessary to maintain the meter.

3   ORM has the speaker sharpening the pencil, but then why would she give it back to the vendor only for him to dull the point in line six?

5   This line presents several difficulties. "Estallar" is generally intransitive but here has an object in "ideas" (which cannot be the subject of any surrounding verbs, all in singular form). The subject of the verb "saltó" could be "him" (the vendor) or the pencil lead (or land mine). "Saltó" could also mean "tripped" or "exploded" if we take "mina" to mean "land mine." An alternative reading that is more grammatical: "The exploding land mine jumped [or skipped] over ideas."

6   ORM translates "despuntólo" as "sharpened the point," whereas I can only find "despuntar" (used transitively) defined as blunting a sharp point or blade — unless "despuntar," like "estallar," is an intransitive verb made transitive: "and again the sad angel made it excel/stand out/sprout/dawn."

7   "Él" could be "him" rather than the pencil.

8   "Lo arrió" is figurative and could be "hauled it down" (as in a sail or a flag), but I use "struck it" (a nautical term — among many that Storni employs — that could also have a stage set for its object). The phrase could also mean "inundated it" or "flooded it" (also typical of Storni's interest in water), but both of these verbs imply action *within* their objects rather than *on* them, and so seem odd followed by "from my memory." "Flushed it from my memory" would work but seems incongruous with the subject "a face of high bronze."

12   ORM has simply, "A vehicle / lifted me with violence," but I think "cualquier" imparts a sense of depersonalizing randomness or even nihilism.

A Hen

1   MF has "under the water," but that would be "bajo el agua."
5   "No está la mente para" is an uncommon construction, but it functions elegantly here.
10   MF has "bustles," but "polizón" seems to mean chiefly "stowaway" or "wanderer."

A Tooth

1   This stanza seems to have had all its commas – and perhaps one or two small words – erased.
2   The compound adverb "solo hacia el cielo" is unusual.
3   Unclear what "tierra adentro" modifies and what this line means.
5   It does seem that the tooth, in its olive/grape/sugar press (the mouth?), goes around the world, rather than the world's turning around in the tooth's press. This would be clearer with "dio la vuelta al mundo" rather than "el mundo." As is typical in this book, the implied subject of each sentence is one particular noun in the title of the poem: hence the repetition of "it" and "its."
6   "Agostar" can also mean "plow under after the harvest."
7   Here "él" could refer to the tooth or the sugar/olive/wine press.
8   "Rice" in an italic font is a surprising image. This stanza seems to be a description of eating from the point of view of the tooth but also carries the idea of many teeth devouring the produce of fields around the world, leaving them bare (echoing "Locusts" in this volume).
9   Unclear whether the tooth or the globe (map? hot air balloon? ball of candy?) causes the trouble. Here again, "it" could be the fixed subject (the tooth) or the actor introduced in this stanza (the globe).
10   "Dar guerra" is "to make difficulties," not necessarily "to make war."
14   "Moliera" seems to be a literary use of the imperfect subjunctive in place of pluperfect.

A Tear

This poem echoes Storni's well-known "Cuadrados y ángulos" ("Squares and Angles"), which ends with a tear in the shape of a square or cube.

1   Unclear whether this line refers to Queen Merope in the Oedipus story. Also unclear whether the tear *was* the stepmother of Oedipus or the result of her weeping.

2   OP capitalizes the initial "y" of this line (perhaps to make clear that the second line is a separate clause) though this is inconsistent with the conventions of the rest of the book (and contrary to VD).

8   "Quicklime sandwich" would be silly, so I take "emparedado" to be an adjective.

9   Subject and object are not clear here. Perhaps the form "traspásame" is dictated by the unwanted sing-song quality of "me traspasa su brasa."

10   This alliterative expression could be a set phrase in Spanish, but I don't find it outside Storni.

12   The comma I use in English appears in some online Spanish versions, as it is difficult to imagine that "tálamos de oro" is a continuation of "orbes lacustres" rather than a separate item in a list. "Orbes" could be "worlds" but also seems to refer back to the source of tears, the eyes. A more far-fetched meaning is puffer fish (also called "pez globo" in Spanish), which cannot be entirely dismissed (even though puffer fish live in the sea, not lakes) given Storni's penchant for strange underwater images. "Tálamos de oro" appears in Shakespeare translations (*The Merchant of Venice*) and in Calderón de la Barca (*El mayor monstruo del mundo*).

14   Unclear who/what is lifting/building and whether "levanta" is even a verb ("a rising" perhaps). My best guess is that the speaker sees all of these objects in the microcosm of a tear.

To Mother Poetry

I avoided "My Lady Poetry" and "Madonna Poetry," both of which could be read as funny, and that is not at all the tone of the original. The final stanza's final image of cruelty shocks all the more for completing a gradual relaxation into a balanced, natural rhythm.

1   "Lanzada" can also mean "impetuous" or "forward." The double meaning here seems intentional, with "lanzada" separated from "contra tu tierra" by "pecadora." ORM and MF treat "lanzada" as reflexive ("throw myself"). ORM rearranges the phrases of the first two lines into a more natural-sounding English order, but I retain the original phrasing for its rhythm, uncharacteristically slowed down by commas.

3   I believe "palmas," like the poem's title, refers to religious figures and so took the meaning "fronds" rather than having the army consist of whole palm trees. Other relevant senses of the word: applause, glories or triumphs.

8   ORM has "barks against you, even if blameless," which avoids saying whether "blameless" refers to the speaker, her audience or the river of lusts. With "urges me guiltlessly on against you," MF would seem to propose that the river is the blameless one. I prefer to think that the speaker is characterizing the river as irrational in its barking. "Sin culpa alzada" in the end is difficult to interpret in this context and seems little used outside Storni.

9   ORM and MF rearrange phrases here as well, but I have kept the original phrasing for the pleasing line breaks it supports.

14   "Cuando nacida" is an unusual phrasing.

www.ingramcontent.com/pod-product-compliance
Lightning Source LLC
Chambersburg PA
CBHW071510040426
42444CB00008B/1582